THE KENTUCKY FRONTIERSMAN THE CONNECTICUT YANKEE AND LITTLE TURTLE'S GRANDDAUGHTER

A Blending of Cultures

The Story of
William Wells and Sweet Breeze
and
Their Descendants

Marilyn Van Voorhis Wendler

HERITAGE BOOKS
2007

HERITAGE BOOKS
AN IMPRINT OF HERITAGE BOOKS, INC.

Books, CDs, and more—Worldwide

For our listing of thousands of titles see our website
at
www.HeritageBooks.com

Published 2007 by
HERITAGE BOOKS, INC.
Publishing Division
65 East Main Street
Westminster, Maryland 21157-5026

Copyright © 1997, 2003 Marilyn Van Voorhis Wendler

All rights reserved. No part of this book may be reproduced or transmitted in any form or by any means, electronic or mechanical, including photocopying, recording or by any information storage and retrieval system without written permission from the author, except for the inclusion of brief quotations in a review.

International Standard Book Number: 978-0-7884-2483-1

CONTENTS

Foreword	v.
Introduction	vii.
Chapter One	1
Chapter Two	53
Chapter Three	67
Chapter Four	97
Chapter Five	112
Footnotes	117
For Further Reading	122

FOREWORD

History is the story of people, their relationships with one another and their environment. It seeks to connect the past with the present and looks for those threads that hold things together or connect things to today.

Marilyn Wendler has chosen three lives as the focus of a story that runs through five generations. The thread is woven through the lives and love of people from a variety of cultures. It presents to the reader an understanding of the non-political history of the Maumee Valley and four people who played a significant role in its development into the contemporary world.

The story is easy to follow and fulfills a real need in understanding the blending of cultures that occurs on the frontier. It gives a vivid illustration of the problems encountered by those who intermarried and lived on the frontier.

It makes the reader understand there was much more on the frontier than conflict of cultures. It is a positive contribution to the social history of the times.

Randall Buchman

INTRODUCTION

This is the story of three generations of a frontier family and the parts they played in the cultural, social and economic development of what was known in the late eighteenth and early nineteenth century as the "far West." It begins with the conflict between two civilizations - one Native American and the other a new class of American pioneers eager to expand their boundaries into formerly forbidden lands.

The role played by frontiersman, William Wells including his friendship with the great Miami Chief Little Turtle and ultimately his marriage to the chief's daughter, Sweet Breeze provides the backdrop for this saga about an extraordinary family with roots firmly planted in two separate cultures.

William Wells, the progenitor, is a familiar name in frontier literature. He has been characterized as cowardly, traitorous, dishonest, illiterate, hot tempered and choleric. Many of these charges come from biographers of Tecumseh, the famed Shawnee warrior who harbored a natural tribal enmity toward Chief Little Turtle of the Miami and was suspicious of Well's influence with the Chief. Philosophical differences concerning measures for dealing with the loss of their lands to the advancing Americans also separated the two leaders. While Tecumseh determined to eradicate all vestiges of white "civilization," Little Turtle and Wells advocated accommodation. Other accusations are based on the correspondence of John Johnston, as easterner who made no secret of his dislike for Wells, and Secretary of War, Henry Dearborn who had arranged for Johnston's appointment to

Fort Wayne and who was not without his own critics. To his own disadvantage, however, Wells exemplified the traits of the typical frontiersman which most easterners disdained. He was hotheaded, impatient, independent and proud of his physical prowess. But most offensive to white society was the fact that he had not only survived his kidnaping but that he had lived among the Indians without making any apparent effort to escape and that he remained close to his friend, Chief Little Turtle, even after he had left the Miami. Moreover, he had chosen a wife among the Indians, not once, but twice. That his wife, Sweet Breeze, daughter of Little Turtle, enjoyed a life made easier by the labor of slaves likely prompted some of the criticism among the New Englanders.

Johnston's accusations that Wells cheated or defrauded the government were never confirmed and Wells continued to enjoy the respect of Generals Anthony Wayne and James Wilkinson and ultimately, in spite of sporadic disagreements, William Henry Harrison. He also had the acceptance and support of his Kentucky family and friends, such as Senator John Pope. His alleged transgressions did not prevent him from marrying a young woman from a prominent Kentucky family who was willing to follow him to the edge of civilization where she would become stepmother to his four children by Sweet Breeze and give birth to three more offspring. As a patriarch who his daughters would later refer to as "our dear deceased father " he insured that his children were and trained to take their place in society even if it meant leaving them in the care of their Kentucky relatives for prolonged periods of time. Throughout his adult life attempts would be made to paint Wells as a villain but he was destined to die a hero's death. As late as 1877, his champions, with the support of his grandson,James M. Wolcott, rallied in protest when it was learned that Wells Street in Chicago, the last tangible monument to his heroism and tragic death was scheduled to be renamed.

Historian Paul Hutton and others have fully documented Well's military exploits and service under Anthony Wayne and to date, Paul Harvey Carter has given the most balanced account of Wells and his friend and mentor, Chief Little Turtle. My challenge was to search beyond the public persona through his interrelationships with family and friends. Well's conversations with Volney, for example, provide a deeper insight into his highly criticized changes in loyalty. Behind the opportunistic "turncoat," as has been charged, is a man who is a realist and who sees value in both the American and Native American cultures. As Carter points out, both Little Turtle and Wells believed that a lasting peace could be accomplished by bringing the two cultures together. The children of Wells and Sweet Breeze would become the instruments through which this goal would ultimately be achieved.

Well's legacy would be perpetuated through his daughters and their descendants. With Mary's marriage to James Wolcott, a "Connecticut Yankee," she bridged the cultural gap. Wolcott was typical of the eastern entrepreneurs who flocked into the Maumee Valley hoping to make a fortune in western lands. With Mary beside him (and her substantial dowry in hand), his vision finally drew him to the Foot of the Rapids on the lower Maumee River. Here he joined in the great city building mania spreading throughout Northwest Ohio. The lives of James and Mary would be inextricably intertwined with the major forces which shaped the trans-Appalachian West in the early nineteenth century. Although unnoticed by most biographers and historians of the era, Mary and James Wolcott and their descendants made lasting contributions to the culture and history of the lower Maumee Valley. Their monument to posterity is the Wolcott House, a tangible symbol of the cultural legacy of Mary's forbears and their conviction that two civilizations could live together in harmony. Marilyn V. Wendler

Chapter I

WILLIAM WELLS

THE KENTUCKY FRONTIERSMAN

Young William Wells set off on a hunting trip with three companions, William and Azael Linn and Nicholas Breashers, sons of neighboring settlers along Beargrass Creek, in the spring of 1784. As the boys traded tales of the game they hoped to bring back to the settlement it would never in the broadest stretch of their imagination occur to them that before the day was over, fourteen year old William would be thrust into a major role in a great historical drama already unfolding upon the frontier of the Northwest Territory. Born at Jacobs Creek, Pennsylvania in 1770, Wells was next to the youngest in a family already hardened by life on the trans-Appalachian frontier. The father, Captain Samuel Wells, a Virginia veteran of the French and Indian War likely served in the British campaign to capture Fort Duquesne (renamed Fort Pitt) at the forks of the Ohio and Monongahela Rivers in 1758, possibly as a member of Captain Thomas Bullitt's valiant Virginia provincial militia. Following the British conquest of the French and their Indian allies in 1760, Wells uprooted his large family from the security of their Virginia homeland to follow the stream of emigrants into the harsh environment of Western Pennsylvania where lands were opening up for settlement.

    Speculative interest soon shifted south of the Ohio River to the traditional Indian hunting grounds, setting the stage for over two decades of bloodthirsty warfare over control of the Ohio Valley. Undaunted by threats of Indian hostility or reports of an impending break with the mother country, Captain Bullitt turned his attention southward to lead an exploratory trip into the heart of Indian territory. He arrived at the falls in 1773. He was followed by fellow Virginian, Colonel John Floyd, commissioned to lay out a town plat (Louisville) for Lord Dunmore, royal governor of Virginia. It is not known whether Captain Wells accompanied Bullitt on this initial trip, but in 1775 and again in 1776, in spite of the now fully blown War for Independence raging in the East, sons Samuel, Jr. and Hayden followed Bullitt's trail into the "Can-tuk-kee" wilderness. Their hardy group expanded Bullitt's survey, covering nearly 10,000 acres and staying in hastily erected cabins for several months each time. They returned home with exciting reports of lands for the taking in Virginia's newest county. In 1779, unable and unwilling to stop the flow of western settlers, the Virginia Legislature confirmed claims for service in the French and Indian War and more recent militia service in the Continental Army for Virginia veterans. Thus encouraged, Samuel and his sons determined to strike out for the "dark and bloody ground."

    To embark upon this hazardous journey into the wilderness, the Wells family - which included in addition to nine year old William, brothers Samuel, Hayden, Yelverton, Peyton, Charles; and sisters Margaret and Elizabeth - joined forces with other former Virginians whose service in the late war entitled them to Kentucky lands. Brother Carty and family would join them after their arrival. Colonel William Oldham, under whom Wells had earned a commission in the Continental Army, was among the travelers as was Colonel William Pope and numerous members of his family. All shared a vision of establishing towns within Bullitt's original survey which would become flourishing centers of commerce and trade . [1]

After several weeks of traveling down the Ohio River in flatboats, a feat rendered more dangerous by bands of Indians who lurked along the river shores to attack straggling boating parties, the hardy group of migrants arrived at the "falls" (near Louisville) where Colonel Floyd, now a seasoned frontiersman, had already established Floyd's Station nearby. Upon arrival,

Pope and Oldham staked their claims near the plat of Louisville. Wells and his sons moved further inland along the Beargrass Creek. Here they built several cabins surrounded by a fortified enclosure, to be known as Wells Station.

White settlements quickly spread throughout the former Indian hunting grounds prompting the tribes above the Ohio River to attack isolated "stations." The earlier settlements of James Harrod, Benjamin Logan, and Daniel Boone had long been the target of Indian harassment and the attacks soon expanded to include the most recently established. Soon after the Wells party's arrival, Colonel John Bowman led an offensive against the Shawnee villages at old Chillicothe (near Xenia, Ohio) in an attempt to discourage further Indian and British raids from across the Ohio. This action resulted in the death of Shawnee Chief, Black Fish and served to intensify the resentment of the Indians. The following summer, a force of a three hundred Indians, representing several tribes, and accompanied by British and Canadians under command of British Captain Henry Byrd and numbering nearly one thousand in all, swept into Kentucky. They forced the surrender of Ruddell's station but Byrd was unable to restrain the anger of the warriors. The inhabitants were either massacred or made prisoner. The combined forces moved on to Martin's Station where over one hundred captives were taken. Bounty and prisoners were ferried back across the Ohio River. As fear and outrage spread across the frontier, Major George Rogers Clark, headquartered at the falls, had little trouble conscripting a force of one thousand backwoodsmen to retaliate against the Indian towns at Chillicothe and Piqua. Wells Station was spared but it is likely that Wells and his older sons joined the militia formed under the unit led by friend and neighbor, Captain John Floyd.

Although Clark's raid provided a temporary respite, sporadic bands of warriors continued to harass the settlements. In the summer of 1781, the inhabitants of Squire Boone's station, near Shelbyville, left their shelter to find a stronger fortification in the Beargrass region. They were attacked before reaching their destination. Colonel Floyd gathered a group of volunteers, including Samuel Wells and his son, Samuel Wells, Jr., to rescue the survivors. Floyd's force was ambushed and half of his men, including Captain Wells were killed in the encounter. Floyd was wounded and his horse shot from underneath him. Samuel Wells, Jr. not only survived but distinguished himself as a hero by placing Floyd on his own mount and running alongside to support the Colonel until they reached safety.

. With the loss of Captain Wells, the children were left without parents . Their mother, Elizabeth Hayden Wells had died soon after giving birth to daughter, Elizabeth. However, sudden death was not a stranger in frontier communities and neighbors relied heavily on one another when tragedy struck. William was befriended by the family of Captain Well's old comrade, William Pope, who had taken over the guardianship of the Linn brothers, also orphaned at a young age. At age ll, he was expected to shoulder his share of responsibility and would be viewed as an "extra rifle" in times of crisis. By frontier standards, young boys were considered men by age 12. They were skilled in the use of weapons and could fight and hunt alongside their elders. They were depended upon to protect their families when fathers and older brothers were gone on military expeditions or extended hunting trips. Thus, it was not unusual that William and his friends would venture the six miles to Roberts Pond to hunt game on that spring morning in 1784. The hunt was successful and several animals, including a bear cub, were killed. As the boys were loading their bounty, they momentarily put their guns aside. While they joked and boasted of their prowess, a small Indian war party had been quietly watching from behind the tall grass. The warriors quickly realized that the that the young hunters were off guard and easily overwhelmed them. They took their captives across the Ohio River and to the towns on the White River in Indiana. Well's three companions were left with the Delaware and later escaped back to Kentucky. Wells, however, was taken to a small Miami village located on the Eel River. Here he was placed in the home of the head chief, Kaweahatta, The Porcupine. He was later adopted by Porcupine and his wife, an elderly couple who wished for a son. Wells related that he developed an affection for his adopted parents who treated him well, and he referred to Kahweahatta as a "sensible man" and a great chief with more influence than any other man in the Wabash country. [2]

Well's new family gave him the name, Apekonite, a Miami term for wild bean, wild potato or wild carrot. This name presumably was chosen because of Well's distinctive red hair which was conspicuous among the dark haired Miami youth. Lieutenant Thomas Hunt, who first met Wells in 1796, recalled the frontiersman's freckled face and winning smile. After several years with the Miami, William developed a deep tan, making him almost indistinguishable, except for the red hair, from his companions. When Count Constantin Volney visited the United States, he had several interviews with Chief Little Turtle and Wells. Volney observed that Well's complexion was unlike most American but resembled that of a ham, "smoke dried, cleaned, and shining." [3]

Wells quickly fit into the Indian way of life. In many ways it was little different than that he left behind. In later years, William was often asked how he could abandon his earlier life with seemingly so little regret. Volney raised this topic in his interview. When asked why so many young captives chose to remain with their captors and preferred the Indian lifestyle to "civilized life," Wells concurred with Volney's observations that the "excessive liberty it allows children in running, playing, and amusing themselves, is much more pleasing. . . than the confinement of schools." Idleness was accepted in Indian society and Volney noted that although it required years to "contract habits of labour and study," it took only a few days to adopt habits of "idleness and independence." [4] William possessed a natural intelligence and readily learned the Miami language and customs. As a young man without parents and only older brothers to rely upon, Wells had learned to survive on his own. This experience would serve him well as a hunter and eventually, a warrior. As he absorbed himself in his new life, his memories of family gradually faded.

As Wells neared manhood, he was occasionally allowed to accompany the Miami war parties. He later admitted to John Johnston, who would become his sworn enemy, that he served as a decoy to lure small boats to the shore of the Ohio River and thus enable the Indians to attack the inhabitants. Most early sources agree that Wells probably accompanied Little Turtle's forces when they successively repelled General Josiah Harmar's march into the Indian country in 1790 and it was at this time that the young captive came to the notice of the great chief.

Meanwhile, William's brothers had little success in discovering his whereabouts. Eventually, Colonel John Hamtramck, American commander at Vincennes, made contact with William, who occasionally visited the fort as an interpreter for his Miami companions. Carty Wells was then living at Coxe's fort, near Bardstown, making a living as a trader and supplier. He often made trips to Vincennes and occasionally carried dispatches for Colonel Hamtramck. During one of these visits in 1788, Hamtramck disclosed that William was alive and living with the Miami at Kenapakomoko, Porcupine's village. Soon after, in January, 1789, Carty made the dangerous trip up the Wabash River to the Eel River village to meet his younger brother for the first time in four years. The trip proved to be futile. William, wary of Carty's motives, claimed that he was not sure he recognized his brother and that he had no interest in returning to Kentucky. He did, however, indicate that he might listen to Samuel. Discouraged, Carty returned to Louisville and related the news to his brothers. Within a few months, Samuel made the trip into the Miami country and met with more successful results. William not only recognized him but agreed to pay a visit to Samuel's home in Louisville. Within a short time, William made good on his promise and arrived in Louisville accompanied by several young Miami braves. The prodigal brother received a warm welcome from Samuel's family. By then, Samuel was already acquiring social and economic prominence. He hoped that this visit with his family on their comfortable "plantation" would convince his brother to break his Miami ties and resume his former lifestyle. William, however, was cordial but could not be swayed. After a few days as a guest in Samuel's home, he returned to his Eel River village. A significant factor in his return was a young Wea woman who was waiting for him in Kenapakomoko. Although William appeared to reject his brother lifestyle, the experience nevertheless must have made a deep impression upon him. It was probably at this time that he first began to have doubts about his role among the Miami. It would also influence the way in which he would rear his own children many years later, impressing upon them the values of education and the importance of adapting to white society.

    Soon after Wells returned to the Miami, the sporadic raids and counter raids that had characterized the frontier for several years, erupted into full scale warfare. President George Washington earlier sent General Josiah Harmar to wipe out Indian resistance at Kekionga (present day Fort Wayne). Little Turtle and his warriors were ready for Harmar and turned the expedition into a shambles. The following year, 1791, General Arthur St. Clair, governor of the Northwest Territory, assembled a force of two thousand and made preparations to make a final assault against the Indians of the Miami Valley. Before the expedition set off, St. Clair sent a smaller force under Captain James Wilkinson to attack the

Eel River village of Kenapakomoko, where Well's Miami family resided. Wells and the Porcupine had left with supplies and ammunition for the defense of Kekionga when the attack occurred. thirty-four women and children, including William's wife, new baby and adoptive mother were taken prisoner.

The attack on the Miami villages only hardened the resolve of Little Turtle and his allies to vanquish the Americans. Warriors from all corners of the Northwest Territory began to gather in the Maumee Valley to resist an anticipated invasion. Meanwhile, the relationship between Wells and Little Turtle was developing into a bond of friendship, trust, and admiration. Little Turtle was increasingly aware of Well's value as a link with the white man's world, as well as his prowess as a warrior, and as proof of that respect, allowed Wells to marry his daughter, Sweet Breeze. Wells was already married, but his wife and child were still in captivity and Miami custom did not prohibit taking a second wife. The marriage of William Wells and Sweet Breeze, or Wakapanke, may have been a union of political convenience, not too unlike that of the legendary Pocahontas and John Rolfe over a century earlier. Little Turtle, even while resisting the military advance of the Americans, recognized the advantages of bridging the two cultures. Whether politically or romantically inspired, the marriage would prove lasting until the untimely death of Sweet Breeze, and their descendants would continue to close the cultural gap between the two civilizations.

In the fall of 1791, St. Clair began his cumbersome march into Indian territory. The expedition was doomed from the beginning. A late start, untrained troops, incompetent or dishonest quartermasters and bad weather were only a few of the problems that would plague St. Clair's army. President Washington had hoped to bolster the army by issuing a call for 1000 militia but only 300 responded. Among the volunteers were Samuel Wells, Jr. and Charles Wells.

The American army finally moved out from Fort Washington in early September, 1791. After building fortifications at Fort Hamilton and Fort Jefferson, the troops reached the present day site of Fort Recovery on November 3, where they established Fort St. Clair Several days earlier, St. Clair made the mistake of sending Major John Hamtramck 's regiment in pursuit of a band of approximately 60 deserters and to protect an advancing supply train, thus weakening the strength of the already diminished regular army. Little Turtle's warriors and scouts followed Hamtramck's movements with great interest and promptly reported the American activity to their chief. Little Turtle's astute leadership had served his warriors well in prior campaigns. Putting his bold strategy into action he ordered an attack against the unsuspecting Americans before they broke camp. The warriors surrounded the camp on the morning of November 4, taking the army totally by surprise. William Wells and several Miami warriors were assigned to pick off the artillery gunners. After almost three hours of hand to hand combat, St. Clair ordered a retreat and the remnants of the American army fled the field. When Little Turtle prohibited his warriors from pursuing the fleeing Americans, the victors returned to plunder the fallen bodies and abandoned equipment littering the camp ground. Among the equipment left behind by the Americans were the six cannon, which due to their cumbersome size, were hidden rather than moved by the warriors. This fact would be recalled by William Wells several years later, to the American advantage.

    The loss of St. Clair's army was one of the worst defeats in American military history. Of the 1400 men encamped on that November morning, 637, including 68 officers were killed. Only three of the thirty three women camp followers survived. In addition to the cannon, nearly $33,000 worth of supplies and equipment was lost. Samuel and Charles Wells escaped back to Kentucky but Colonel Oldham was among the dead.

During the heat of the battle, William Wells was probably unaware of the presence of his brothers and the colonel, but likely learned of their participation in a later visit with Samuel. The possibility that he and his brothers might meet as adversaries could hardly have escaped his attention and may have been a factor in his later decision to cast his lot with the Americans. Other concerns were also pressuring Wells to re-examine his position. He recognized that he would have a better chance to secure the release of his Miami family as a representative of white society. Perhaps after discussing the issue with Little Turtle and Porcupine, he accompanied his foster father and a delegation of Miami to Vincennes where Colonel Hamtramck had re-established his command. The Miami delegation hoped to negotiate the release of the prisoners but Hamtramck lacked the authority. He urged Wells to await the arrival of General Rufus Putnam, head of a commission recently appointed to conclude a peace treaty with the tribal nations.

Wells agreed to wait for Putnam and in the meantime, he met again with Samuel, who had traveled to Vincennes in hopes of bringing William home with him. When the Miami chiefs returned to their villages, William accompanied his brother to Louisville. This visit was longer than the previous one and William was more open to the opportunities to be gained by returning to his former home. He later explained to Volney, that although the freedom of the Indian lifestyle still held a great attraction for him, his Indian comrades lived entirely in the present. Sweet Breeze was expecting their first child and William was concerned about the future of his new family. He wanted his wife to share in the relative comforts and conveniences enjoyed by his sister-in-law rather than the austere existence experienced by most Miami women, upon whose shoulder fell all the responsibilities of household affairs, caring for children and animals alike and who were "literally beasts of burden." William was beginning to envision the advantages of establishing a farm like his brothers and bringing up children who "when you are worn out with old age, will gently close your eyes." [5] When referring to Well's change of heart during this period, some critics argue that the frontiersman conveniently switched sides and joined the American forces when he saw the tides of war turning against the Indian nations. However, his conversations with Volney, his actions prior to offering his services to General Anthony Wayne, and especially his enduring friendship with Little Turtle and their joint efforts to bring about peace before and after Wayne's decisive campaign tend to prove otherwise.

Putnam did not arrive at Fort Washington, where the Miami prisoners were being held, until July. He immediately sent for Wells to act as interpreter. Wells readily agreed to serve for one dollar a day although he was probably prepared to offer his services at any price in order to accomplish the release of his former neighbors and family members from Kenapakomoko. Shortly after arrival, William was reunited with his Miami foster mother, wife and son "amid many tears" according to observers. For Wells this was a critical moment in which he was faced with the decision of whether to maintain two families or to cut his ties with his first wife, now that he had secured her release. Evidence seems to indicate that he followed the latter course and the only reference to this first union is in 1807 when Wells reveals the recent loss of a son.

The captives, estimated to be around one hundred in number, were loaded onto five barges accompanied by Wells, General Putnam with sixty soldiers and, as a peace emissary, Moravian missionary, John Heckewelder. The flotilla set off for Vincennes on August 16. Heckewelder was fascinated with the former captive and recorded for posterity an incident which occurred during the trip. Wells employed his skills as a hunter to keep the army supplied with meat. Somewhere along the way he encountered a bear, which he wounded but did not kill with his first shots. According to one account, Wells had learned from the Miami the ancient technique of subduing large animals, such as the bear, by intimidation. Thus, Wells after approaching the wounded animal and striking it on the nose, chastised the bear for whimpering. Knowing the fortunes of war, Wells reasoned, "he ought to die like a hero and not like an old woman" and added that if the situation were reversed, he (Wells) would die with "firmness and courage, as became a true warrior."[6] Well's belief in this code of war would be demonstrated almost twenty years later when he faced his own death while defending the soldiers and civilians at Fort Dearborn. It also illustrates how thoroughly Wells had absorbed the Miami culture as a young man growing up under the tutelage of the Miami warriors.

Upon reaching Vincennes, Putnam officially released the prisoners and negotiations were begun with the Wabash and Eel River Miami. Thirty-one chiefs signed the peace treaty in September of 1792, but all refused to recognize the legitimacy of any white settlements above the Ohio River. This, of course would not be accepted by the Americans who already had settlements at Marietta, Columbia and Losantiville (Cincinnati), and Gallipollis along the Ohio River and settlers were even then moving into the hinterland to carve out new cities in the wilderness.

Meanwhile, there was unrest among the Wabash Miami who had not supported the treaty. The inhabitants of Kekionga, encouraged by British agents Matthew Elliot and Alexander McKee moved to the Auglaize (Defiance) where several Shawnee and Pottawattomi villages were already established and where they would be nearer the protection of Canada if hostilities should break out. Little Turtle moved his family, including Sweet Breeze, to this new location, known as Little Turtle's Village, in the summer of 1792. While the men talked of war and made preparations for fall hunting, the women and children planted and cultivated extensive fields of corn along the banks of the Auglaize and Maumee Rivers.

Still hoping to persuade the remaining tribes to enter into peace negotiations, Putnam convinced Wells to accept an assignment as a peace envoy to the Kekionga Miami and the the Delaware for the sum of $300. Although torn between his loyalty to the Miami and the realization that they would ultimately have to accommodate the American demands, Wells agreed to travel to Kekionga to invite the tribes to meet in council and to gather information on their activities. If successful, he would receive an additional $200 bonus. This was a dangerous mission even for Wells. Four former emissaries, including the seasoned frontier soldier, John Hardin, had been killed while attempting to deliver the same message that Wells was now entrusted with. William left Vincennes in October, 1792 and after finding that Little Turtle and Sweet Breeze had left Kekionga, traveled on to the Auglaize.. For several months, the Americans had no word of his whereabouts, causing Putnam to fear that he might be dead. However, he apparently took this opportunity to spend some time with Sweet Breeze while under the protection of his father-in-law, Little Turtle. It was during this period that Wells made the acquaintance of a young Indian captive, Oliver Spencer in a nearby Shawnee village. Twelve year old Oliver was nearly the same age that Wells had been when he was carried off to live with the Miami and the older man likely felt a twinge of sympathy for the youngster's situation. Spencer later related that Wells inquired about his parents and their whereabouts and that this information was later passed on to Hamtramck at Vincennes, who arranged for his eventual return to his family.

    It may also have been during this period that Wells and Little Turtle discussed their new relationship and its implications. According to family tradition related by Well's great nephew, Nathan Heald, the two men agreed to a compact wherein each would go their own way. Their friendship would remain firm and they would continue to work together to ease the Indian/White impasse'. This differs from a more popular version in which they agree to kill each other if they should meet in battle. The latter version apparently originated in Fort Wayne and was repeated by William Wells Wolcott over one hundred years later, when he was seventy-three years old. This version is less likely, as demonstrated by their cooperation and steadfastness of purpose throughout their lifetimes. The two men may also have discussed problems of a more domestic nature. Wells would be understandably concerned abut the safety and welfare of his wife. The couple's first child, a daughter named Anne, namesake of his brother Samuel's daughter, Ann, was born in 1792 or early 1793, the period in which Wells remained at the Auglaize.

    Wells presented his offers of a peace council to the various tribes in January and was disappointed but not surprised at their rejection. He relayed his information to Hamtramck and apparently returned to his family, as he was not seen again until August 1793. At this time, Hamtramck requested that Wells return to the Auglaize where at the urging of the British agents, McKee and Elliot, a large council was convening. This conference was of sufficient importance that a three man American commission was sent to negotiate with the tribes on the lower Maumee River. Both the Indians and the Americans appeared willing to make peace if their respective demands were met. The British agents, however, continued to impress the Indians with their promised support and McKee stepped up his efforts to supply them with arms and ammunition from his post at the Foot of the Rapids (lower Maumee River). The Indians reiterated their demands for the Ohio River as a boundary to white settlement and the conference ended in a deadlock. Wells returned to Fort Washington where General Anthony Wayne was anxiously waiting for word of the negotiations before taking any military action. Wells reported to Wayne in September, warning him that the Legion would face over 1500 warriors from many tribes, all well armed and supplied by the British. [7]

Well's mission aptly demonstrated his usefulness as a spy and prompted Wayne to give him command of a unit of scouts to accompany the army on its march into Indian territory. The company consisted of about twenty men, including Nicholas Miller and William Polk, who like Wells were former captives and Robert McClellan, a veteran frontiersman. William escorted his wife and child to the safety of his brother Samuel's home in Louisville before joining up with Wayne's army. Samuel, meanwhile had been appointed a major in the Kentucky Mounted volunteers and Charles soon enlisted under Colonel Butler at Louisville.

Wayne built a series of forts at intervals along the route earlier taken by St. Clair. The last of these was built at the site of the former general's disastrous defeat. While the army moved northward, Wells and his men scouted the countryside and took several prisoners in hopes of convincing them to divulge information about the morale and whereabouts of the enemy. Wells and his company proved invaluable assets to Wayne. Dressed as Indians and fluent in many tribal dialects, they were able to pass through Indian territory undetected. On one occasion, Wells came upon his foster father, Porcupine, but recognized him in time to prevent a fatal confrontation. Wells continued to hope that war could be avoided, going so far as to release two hostages, a woman and child, to return to their village carrying the message that negotiations were still a viable possibility. The other captives, Charles Wells, now a member of the group, recalled that the remaining captives were taken to Vincennes for interrogation.[8] Wayne agreed to a 30 day truce, providing time for the release of all American prisoners. When no reply was received, Wayne again sent Wells to gather information. The scouts came upon a small party encamped along the Auglaize River. Two of the warriors were shot while McClellan overpowered the third.

To everyone's amazement, the subdued warrior was found to Christopher Miller, the younger brother of Nicholas, who had remained with the Shawnee. Christopher revealed that the Indians had agreed to accept Wayne's offer but had been dissuaded by McKee, Elliot and Simon Girty.

Although General Wayne remained at his headquarters at Fort Greenville, an advance group had settled in at the former site of Fort St. Clair, renamed Fort Recovery by the Americans. Meanwhile, Little Turtle, Blue Jacket and Buckongehelas had assembled over two thousand warriors at the Auglaize. Little Turtle planned to attack the American supply lines and isolate the forts. On June 29, a supply train reached Fort Recovery and successfully deposited its cargo. As it departed the following day, it was attacked and pillaged by the waiting Indians. The commanding officer and about fifteen of his men were killed and approximately three hundred pack horses were captured. Encouraged by their success, the warriors determined to attack the stockade. This decision would prove costly. Wells had earlier revealed the hiding places of St. Clair's lost cannon to Putnam and this information had been passed on to General Wayne. The artillery pieces were relocated within the blockhouse and as the warriors charged, they were repulsed by cannon fire before they could reach the enclosure. The Indians made two attempts to reduce the stockade, but gave up the following day and returned to the Glaize. This defeat, although not costly in lives, was demoralizing to the loosely knit confederacy who believed their united forces would easily overwhelm the Americans. Many followed the lead of the departing lake tribes and returned home. Little Turtle recognized that his warriors could not hope to win a total victory without stronger support from the British, and with that not forthcoming, counseled against further military encounters. Anthony Wayne's forces continued to move toward the Maumee River and by August 9, encamped near the confluence of the

Maumee and Auglaize Rivers. Here he began construction of a fortified stockade which he would name Fort Defiance. While construction was underway, Wells and his spies continued to scout the countryside. On August 11, they surveyed Fort Miami at the Foot of the Rapids. On their return, they encountered a small Delaware village Disguised as Indians, they entered the camp and Wells spoke with one of the warriors. They were about to exit when they were suddenly recognized and forced to fight their way out. Well's wrist was shattered by a bullet and McClelland was injured in the shoulder. Charles Wells later claimed that he was present during the incident and received a flesh would in the thigh. They managed to make their escape and were rescued by Dragoons summoned by Miller, who had ridden ahead.

    Wayne made one last effort for peace and dispatched Christopher Miller to the camps with a flag of truce. The Indians countered by asking Wayne to remain at Fort Defiance Wile they conferred. It was at this time that Little Turtle supposedly made his eloquent plea to his own people to sue for peace and referred to Wayne as the "chief who never sleeps." The younger warriors were not disposed to follow his advice and dismissed him as a coward, forcing Little Turtle to resign as leader of the Indian confederacy in favor of the Shawnee Chief, Blue Jacket. By August 16, Wayne decided to take the initiative and the army advanced down the Maumee River and on to a site later referred to as Fallen Timbers due to the many fallen trees felled by a recent tornado. The Indians, sensing an imminent battle, had fasted for three days and many had slipped back to their camps. After a brief delay at Fort Deposit, Wayne's army resumed the march. They met what remained of the Indian forces at 10:00 A.M. on August 20 and the battle commenced. After little more than an hour, the Indians began to retreat toward the British Fort Miami. The British, however, closed the gates to the fort and left the Indians to fend for themselves. Although neither side suffered great loss of life, the Indian spirit was broken. They had been deceived by the British, who they considered their allies, and their power was proved fallible by Wayne, who added further insult by burning their cornfields stretching along the Maumee. This brief military encounter between the Americans and the confederation of Indian tribes, became known as the Battle of Fallen Timbers and would take on increasing importance as one of the most decisive victories of the American military.

General Wayne returned to Fort Defiance for a few days to reinforce the structure in anticipation of a possible counter move by the British and Indians. He then struck out for Kekionga and the Miami villages in Wabash country. He ordered the construction of a fort on the south bank of the St. Mary's River at the former site of Kekionga and near the confluence of the two rivers. Wayne and the main body of his army marched back to Fort Defiance and on to Greenville where he planned to convene a major peace council the following summer. Colonel Hamtramck assumed command of the fort, which was completed in October and named Fort Wayne.

Wells remained with the army at Fort Wayne as the Miami returned to re-build their villages. It appears that Sweet Breeze, who was expecting her second child, remained in Louisville with her infant daughter, Anne. Meanwhile, Wells and his scouts were assigned to bring in army deserters. This was not a pleasant task, but Wells at least, was well paid by the federal government. They also served as messengers to invite the great chiefs to the upcoming peace council.

The council convened in June, 1795. Over a thousand chiefs and warriors began to assemble in Greenville. Little Turtle did not arrive until June 23 but soon established himself in a leadership role. Wells was appointed chief interpreter and would assist Little Turtle as he debated the terms of peace with Wayne. On August 2, Little Turtle and the Miami and Eel River tribesmen met privately with the General. Little Turtle revealed his intention to live near Fort Wayne and requested that his son-in-law, William Wells be chief interpreter at the fort. Little Turtle is reputed to have said that would be the first to sign the treat and the last to break it. Actually, he was the last of the major chiefs to sign on August 3, 1795.

Well's scouts were disbanded after the treaty signing but, as Little Turtle requested, Wells remained at Fort Wayne. His services had been amply rewarded by the federal government. It is estimated that he earned nearly two thousand dollars between 1793 and 1795. In addition, Wayne wrote to Secretary of War James McHenry in 1796, that Wells "has rendered very essential services to the United States . . . by carrying messages - taking prisoners and gathering intelligence." Wayne referred to the incident in which a bullet had "shattered the bone of his right arm to pieces . . .by which his arm is so much disabled" that he should be entitled to a pension. [9] Accordingly, a pension of twenty dollars per month was agreed upon. Wells settled on a small stream which came to be known as Spy Run, on the site of old Kekionga between the St. Mary and St. Joseph Rivers. Here he built a homestead which would grow to include an orchard and a self sufficient farm. Little Turtle, as he had promised, established a new village about fourteen miles from the fort, which was called Turtletown.

In 1796, Wells and Little Turtle made their first visit to Philadelphia, the nation's capital, and met with President George Washington. The President presented Little Turtle with a ceremonial sword and the Chief who had become something of a celebrity, sat for his portrait by popular artist, Gilbert Stuart. The following year , Wells and Little Turtle again traveled to Philadelphia to meet with new president, John Adams. Wells had continued to press for a position in the Indian Department and this time he was successful. He was appointed interpreter and deputy Indian agent at a salary of three hundred dollars a year. It was during this trip that the two met the French writer, Constantin Volney, who interviewed

Little Turtle through Wells at great length. Volney was also fascinated with William and his experience as a captive. Little Turtle and Wells remained in Philadelphia throughout the winter, discussing and promoting their "civilization" program. They planned to gradually convince and educate the Miami to adopt an agrarian lifestyle, financing the program through government annuities and sale of some Miami lands. They left in the spring, confident that federal officials were in agreement with their ideas, and arrived in Pittsburgh in May. Here they made several purchases, authorized by government agents, which included several shirts for themselves and yards of calico for their wives. They also purchased a number of farming tools to implement their plan. Wells separated from the party on the return trip and stopped by Louisville where he reunited with his wife and two young daughters, Ann and Rebecca. Baby Rebecca was named for his brother Samuel's daughter, Rebecca, whose life William would later save at the Fort Dearborn massacre, losing his own in the effort. The frontiersman turned landholder also obtained a half dozen slaves from his brother Samuel's plantation. After a short visit, the Wells family returned to their new home on Spy Run, which they would later refer to as Wellsington and William, in addition to his duties as agent, would commence the life of a farmer.

 Well's first task was to complete construction of a two story log house to accommodate his growing family. William Wayne, namesake of the General, was born in 1797. General Wayne had passed away in December, 1796 at Fort Presque Ile (Erie, Pennsylvania), following an attack of the gout. Wayne's death was unfortunate for Wells and Little Turtle. The General had great admiration for the abilities of both men and understood their plan to gradually bring the Indians around to an agricultural lifestyle as well as the challenges that they faced in accomplishing that goal. Little Turtle had already begun to adopt some traits of white society. While traveling in the East, he dressed in the style of the Americans, but according to his son-in-law, when he returned home he "must at once resume the Indian dress and habits" in order not to draw suspicion or "wound the pride" of his tribesmen. The government built a log house for Little Turtle in Turtletown and the Chief had acquired "good clothes, tea, and coffee: he has even a cow, and his wife makes butter" but he had to exercise extreme care not to flaunt his worldly goods in the face of his neighbors. Indeed, their disapproval was evidenced when his first cow was mysteriously slaughtered during the night.[10]

In 1796, Well's friend, Colonel Hamtramck, was transferred to Detroit and Major Thomas Hunt assumed command at Fort Wayne. Hunt and Wells were likely well acquainted as both had served under General Wayne. Hunt's seventh child, John Elliot Hunt was born at Fort Wayne in 1798, just two years before the birth of Well's youngest daughter, Mary (Polly) in 1800. Although the Hunt family would move on to Detroit in 1803, Mary Wells and John Hunt would become neighbors twenty-three years later in the frontier community of Maumee City, Ohio. The Hunt family would make another appearance at Fort Wayne in 1805 while en route to a new assignment in St. Louis. Wells had received appointment as Justice of the Peace, due largely to political maneuvering on his behalf by William Henry Harrison, Territorial Governor of Indiana. On June 4, 1805, Wells performed the marriage ceremony for Ruth Hunt and Dr. Abraham Edwards, surgeon's mate at Fort Wayne. Two years later, after the deaths of Major and Mrs. Hunt, John Hunt and his sister, Mary, were brought back to Fort Wayne to stay with the Edwards, where they would become reacquainted with the Wells children.[11]

When Indiana Territory was formed in 1800, Wells temporarily lost his position but was re-appointed by President Thomas Jefferson in 1802 for an annual salary of six hundred dollars plus subsistence pay. Well's responsibilities included distributing annuities, granting licenses to traders, convening councils when needed and generally promoting good relations between the Indians and the American government. Little Turtle had requested that a trading house or "factory" be built in Fort Wayne and that Wells become the "factor." Jefferson complied, but Secretary of War Henry Dearborn, after ordering Wells to oversee the construction, appointed John Johnston, an easterner with political connections, as factor. Johnston and Wells disliked each other from the beginning. Johnston had little empathy for the Indians and he distrusted Wells for his friendship with Little Turtle and the Miami. He continued to plant suspicion and make unsubstantiated charges against the frontiersman to government officials until Well's untimely death. Wells was equally as distrustful of Johnston although the two would necessarily have to work together for nearly a decade. Johnston had strong political ties in the East but Wells was better known in the West. His brother, Samuel, had served in the Kentucky Legislature in 1795, 1796 and 1799 and John Pope, whose family had befriended Wells as a young man, was a United States Senator. Wells also hoped for the support of Governor William Henry Harrison, who had served as aide de camp for Anthony Wayne. The two young men had become friends during that campaign and Harrison had helped Wells with his reading and writing skills. Harrison had described Wells as "a sober, active and faithful public servant" with greater knowledge of Indian language and manners than anyone and he was well aware of Well's influence with Little Turtle.[12] What the two men could not foresee was how their plans for the salvation of the Indians would ultimately clash when friendship succumbed to political loyalties and ambition. Like Wells, Harrison and President Jefferson were convinced that the Indians must adapt an agricultural lifestyle. The men differed on the means to achieve that goal.

    Wells and Little Turtle had met with a group of Quakers including George Ellicott in Baltimore in 1801. They had asked for their support in pressing Congress to pass a resolution prohibiting the sale of liquor to the Indians. Little Turtle was greatly concerned over the issue of drunkenness which was decimating so many of his tribesmen and warned that liquor was more dangerous than the gun or the tomahawk They also discussed their "civilization plan" with the Quakers and requested their aid in teaching the Indians to farm. The Quakers agreed to both requests and promised to send a delegation to Fort Wayne.

Accordingly, on March 29, 1804, Gerald Hopkins, George Ellicott, Joel Wright and Phillip Dennis arrived at Fort Wayne. They carried a letter of introduction from Secretary of War Dearborn to Johnston and Wells. They were met on arrival by John Whipple, fort commander. Whipple directed them to the home of a local trader who provided them quarters for the night. The following morning they again met with the commander who was accompanied by Wells, as agent and factor, Johnston. Both men welcomed the delegation warmly and offered them accommodations in their own homes. They accepted the hospitality of the factor while Wells set off to inform Little Turtle and the Miami of their presence and to invite them to meet at the agent's home to discuss their mission. Thus, on April 4th, the delegation, accompanied by Johnston, finally met with the great chief. During the ensuing conversation, in which Little Turtle described his recent illness with compliments for the kindness of the garrison's physician, (Doctor Edwards) in providing treatment, Wells revealed that the condition was gout. When he had informed the chief that his was the complaint of gentlemen, the Turtle had replied with characteristic humor, "I always thought I was a gentleman." After about an hour of such cordiality, host and guests gathered for an "excellent dinner." Sweet Breeze, assisted by her servant girls had prepared two turkeys, one roasted and one boiled, and a "large supply of cranberry sauce." Williams's wife, who was described by Hopkins as a "modest, well looking Indian woman," departed from Miami tradition and sat at the head of the table, across from her husband, indicating that she too, had adapted to the ways of white society, possibly as a result of time spent with her sister in law.[13] Wells appears to have established a home life for his family as close as possible to that of his Kentucky relatives.

After many more meetings and dinners with the various Miami chiefs, it was agreed that Phillip Dennis would remain to demonstrate the techniques of farming. The Quakers departed on April 15, with Wells and Johnston accompanying them as far as the Foot of the Rapids of the Maumee River.. Throughout the summer, the former warriors showed great interest in Dennis's labor and gathered daily to watch his progress as he cultivated the land set aside for the project. However, they showed no inclination to assist him or to follow his example. Dennis harvested his crops in the fall and returned East, fully aware that he had failed in his mission.

In addition to encountering problems with their "civilization plan," Wells and Little Turtle would suffer a deep personal loss when Sweet Breeze died in late 1804 or early 1805. There is no known reference to the cause of death or to the place of burial. The only description of Sweet Breeze appears to be the one that Quaker, Gerald Hopkins recorded in his journal. Little Turtle had hoped that his daughter would provide a link between his people and the Americans. In this, she succeeded and her children would continue the process. But the substance of the woman remains a shadow, revealed only in her roles as dutiful daughter, wife and mother.

Following the death of their mother, the Wells children returned to Louisville and the home of their uncle, Samuel. The children found a warm welcome in the large family of Samuel and Mary Wells, which included their daughters Mary, Margaret, Rebecca and Ann. Anne and Rebecca formed a close friendship with their cousins, Ann and Rebecca, with whom they shared a name. Mary, commonly referred to as Polly, and only four years old when Sweet Breeze died, was affectionately considered the baby of the family. Samuel took a special interest in seven year old William Wayne, who was somewhat younger than his own sons. The older children, like their cousins, were enrolled in area schools, an advantage they did not have in their former residence. Life in Louisville was a drastic change from Fort Wayne. It was fast becoming a major inland port and by 1806, boasted over three hundred houses and numerous shops, the majority of substantial brick construction as compared to the log architecture the Wells children were familiar with. In addition, the girls were introduced into a more sophisticated social life that contrasted sharply with Fort Wayne which was described as "destitute of society" [14] and characterized by drinking, gambling, card playing and fighting among the soldiers and traders who made up the population of the garrison and nearby area. Anne and Rebecca were not yet old enough to attend the occasional parties and balls with their older cousins, but old enough to relish their descriptions of their social life and to enjoy the preparations surrounding cousin Mary's wedding to James Audrain, member of a prominent Detroit trading family. Meanwhile, "Polly" and Wayne were free to roam the fields and explore the barns and outbuildings on their uncle's plantation.

While William Well's children were enjoying the comparative comfort and freedom of Louisville, Wells and Little Turtle were considering ways to salvage their "civilization" plan. Little Turtle understood that his people would only accept instructions from someone they knew and trusted. Thus, he and Wells proposed a plan to Secretary Dearborn whereby the tribes would be divided into separate settlements and each would be supervised by someone in whom they had confidence. He proposed that some of their government annuities be set aside for the project and suggested that Wells be appointed to coordinate the plan. Instead, the Quakers received a government appropriation of six thousand dollars and one of their own members, William Kirk, was appointed as supervisor. Kirk had visited Fort Wayne the previous year but had not been favorably received by Little Turtle or Wells. Both men were disappointed at Kirk's appointment and Little Turtle was offended when Kirk bypassed Turtletown to establish the center of his agricultural operations at the Pottawatomi village of Five Medals and the Mississinewa Miami under Chief Richardville. In spite of being passed over for the appointment, Wells called a council in May, 1807 and made a futile attempt to convince the Indians to accept Kirk's leadership. Little Turtle and the Miami, however, were adamant in their dislike of Kirk and accused him of stealing the Chief's plan and presenting it as his own. As opposition mounted, Wells urged Kirk to give up his plans to set up the model farms. Kirk and Johnston blamed Wells for the Indian resistance and sent official complaints to Secretary Dearborn, who also condemned Wells for his opposition. Little Turtle and most of the friendly chiefs backed Wells and wrote to President Jefferson expressing their support for the Agent and lack of confidence in Kirk, who they felt had wasted their annuity money. In an effort to appease the Indians, Dearborn transferred Kirk to the Shawnee at Wapakoneta and ultimately dismissed him for misuse of funds in 1808.

    The furor over the civilization plan was just the beginning of a campaign by Johnston to discredit Wells in the eyes of the government and to turn Territorial Governor Harrison against his old friend. More importantly, it masked the growing hostility of the Indians toward white civilization in general and their anger over the government land policies in particular.

    Harrison had made a series of treaties with the various Indian tribes whereby the United States acquired large portions of land throughout Indiana, Illinois and Missouri. The governor was well aware that Wells and Little Turtle were opposed to these land cessions although they had reluctantly played a part in persuading the other tribes to agree to the Treaty of Vincennes in 1803. They recognized the importance of maintaining a good relationship with Harrison and others in authority. Since the lands in question surrounded Vincennes, the territorial capital, they rationalized that this was within the dictates of the Treaty Greenville which Little Turtle had pledged to uphold. Subsequent land cessions heightened the concern of Little Turtle and Wells and the Agent advised the Miami to stand up for their rights when dealing with Governor's emissaries. Wells believed that as Indian Agent, he had a responsibility to the Indians as well as the government. Harrison disagreed and accused Wells of treachery. Johnston used this impasse between the former friends to further discredit Wells. He charged that Wells was illegally supplying the Indians with whiskey, when in fact, the agent was working with Little Turtle to discourage the heavy use of alcohol; that he was illiterate, when letters and documents proved otherwise; and he made a totally unfounded accusation that he was siphoning off government annuities for his own use. Although none of these charges were substantiated, Harrison sent Johnston's letters on to Dearborn who was anxious for an excuse to remove Wells as Indian Agent.

During the summer of 1805, Harrison recognized the need for a more conciliatory approach and convened a council at Grouseland, his official residence at Vincennes. Little Turtle and Richardville were in attendance and Wells acted as official interpreter. In exchange for additional land cessions, each participating tribe received goods totaling one thousand dollars for the larger groups such as the Miami proper, the Delaware and Potawatomi and half that amount to the Wea and the Eel River Miami. Following the Treaty of Grouseland, Harrison met with Wells and Little Turtle and the three were able to resolve many of their differences. The Governor recognized the importance of maintaining their loyalty and raised Well's pay as Indian Agent to seven hundred and fifty dollars a year. The Chief was not overlooked and in addition to raising his pension to one hundred and fifty dollars, the government at this time

agreed to construct a house for him on the Eel River.
Little Turtle and Wells continued to hope for the success of their civilization plan but were increasingly worried over the rising militancy and restlessness of the Indians. They were particularly concerned over rumors circulating about the hostile activities of the Shawnee, Tecumseh and his brother, The Prophet, who were purportedly urging members of the various tribes to convene at their settlement near Greenville, Ohio in direct violation of the Treaty of Greenville. Several thousand Indians passed through the area between 1806 and 1807. Most stopped at Fort Wayne and it was Well's responsibility as Agent to feed and provide for them. With such a large number within a small area, there was always a danger of violence or even a surprise attack on the garrison. Possibly for this reason, Wells continued to leave his children in the care of his brother, Samuel in Louisville. Sometime during this period, Wells became a father again. Jane Wells was born in 1808 to Wells and an unknown Indian Woman. Miami marriages were easily entered into and dissolved and Wells and the mother seem to have parted shortly after the child's birth. Jane is not included in Well's will but was recognized as a half blooded Miami in later treaties.

    By April, 1807, nearly four hundred warriors had crossed the "white boundary to join Tecumseh in Greenville, causing considerable alarm among the settlers of western Ohio and Kentucky. Wells, after a fruitless appeal to Dearborn, expressed his concern to Harrison. This time, Harrison was in complete agreement as to the seriousness of the situation and although he could not intervene in Ohio he addressed the Indian Territorial Assembly and warned of the probability of Indian hostilities in the near future. Wells lacked official backing but sent his friend, Anthony Shane, a Shawnee half-breed who had served under General Wayne, to invite Tecumseh and the Prophet to hear a message from the government at Fort Wayne. Tecumseh countered that Wells must come to him. Shane returned, this time with a message that the Indians must leave Ohio. Tecumseh again repudiated Well's directive and increased his efforts to create an Indian confederacy strong enough to drive out all vestiges of white civilization. He also formed new alliances with the British and Canadians who still hoped to regain control of the Northwest Territory.

Wells continued to keep Dearborn informed of the Indian activities and the dangerous influence of the Prophet, but his messages went unheeded by the Secretary, whose dislike of Wells apparently affected his judgement. Harrison, however, sent a message to the dissidents at Greenville in which he accused the Prophet of collusion with the British and of speaking for the Devil and not for the Great Spirit. He urged them to drive the Prophet out but his message fell on deaf ears.

Indian activity around Greenville died down as fall approached. Tecumseh's followers had ignored their summer hunting and were forced to return to their various agencies to collect their government supplies. Only about one hundred believers remained with the Prophet when he finally moved to a site on the Tippecanoe River, inside Indiana Territory. Wells used this opportunity to encourage the Miami to leave Tecumseh and return home. A large number did return to the protection of Well's agency but both the agent and the factor found it difficult to maintain sufficient supplies. Wells requested extra supplies from the War Department, cautioning that the situation was volatile but again was rebuffed by Dearborn. The Secretary had no sympathy with the Indian's plight and inferred that Wells was only looking for a profit.

Wells realized that Dearborn was more intent than ever to remove him from his post and he requested permission to take a small delegation of Indians to Washington to meet with President Jefferson and other government officials. He also stated in his request that he needed time to visit his family and revealed at this time that he had recently lost a son who was "kild by an accedent (sic) a few days ago." [15] This was an apparent reference to his child by his first wife, as he planned to bring young William Wayne Wells along on this trip. Father, son and grandfather (Little Turtle), accompanied by six other specially chosen chiefs, set off for the Capital in the fall of 1808. Wells hoped that this trip would provide an opportunity for the Indian leaders to express their grievances over Jefferson's land policies to the President himself. He also had a personal interest in meeting with Dearborn to discuss their differences and to make stronger political connections favorable to his position. Jefferson cordially received the delegation, distributed gifts and delivered a short oration in which he offered no support for the Chief's opposition to further loss of their land. Although this meeting must have been an awesome experience for twelve year old Wayne, the mission was a diplomatic failure. Wells was also disappointed in his meeting with Dearborn. He had earlier written to the Secretary pointing out that although all the other agents had housing provided to them by the government, he had not received any such assistance and he now requested that the government furnish him with a new house, as they had done for Johnston. He also reminded the Secretary that he had not received pay for services as Interpreter for Harrison or a number of other duties he had performed. Dearborn not only did not respond to Well's letter, but wrote to Harrison that he had "lost confidence in his integrity." [16] So much in fact, that he was officially removing Wells from his position as Indian Agent. Lacking the courage to personally convey this information to Wells, he wrote a letter of dismissal which he sent on to Johnston with instructions to deliver to Wells on his return.

    Wells and his son separated from the group on the return trip and traveled south to Louisville. Both were anxious to rejoin the family but Wells was also interested in renewing his acquaintance with a young woman he had met at his brother's house on an earlier visit. Mary Geiger was the daughter of Colonel Frederick Geiger, member of a prominent Kentucky

family and friend and neighbor of Samuel Wells. William renewed his courtship and in spite of the great differences in their backgrounds, the couple was married on March 7, 1809, in the presence of family and friends. Undoubtedly, the new Mrs. Wells would have preferred to remain near Louisville, but William had unfinished affairs to attend to in Fort Wayne. After several weeks, William, his new wife, and four children departed for their home at Wellsington. Samuel's daughter, Rebecca, accompanied her uncle's family so that she would have an opportunity to visit her sister, Mary, whose husband, James Audrain had recently opened a trading post near the fort. Romance would blossom when Rebecca was introduced to the thirty-four year old Captain Nathan Heald, commander at Fort Wayne. Heald was immediately attracted to the high spirited Rebecca. John Hunt later recalled that when the Captain was "paying his addresses to Miss Wells," he (Hunt) set up "the marks" for the young couple to fire at and revealed that Rebecca usually "came off best " in the shooting contest. [17]
The Wells family arrived at Fort Wayne on April 9, 1809. Johnston was waiting at the fort with his wedding present - Well's official letter of dismissal and the news that he was taking over Well's agency. It was not in Well's nature to accept this action without a fight. He knew that he had the loyalty of Little Turtle and the chiefs friendly to his ideas. He quickly set about to recruit additional support from Captain Heald, General Harrison and General James Wilkinson, a friend from Wayne's campaign. All agreed to sent letters on his behalf to new Secretary, William Eustis. Harrison, in spite of their earlier differences, was particularly dismayed at Dearborn's action.

    Not satisfied with Well's dismissal, Johnston continued to make disparaging statements about his rival. He played down the reports of Indian hostilities to Eustis, claiming that Wells had planted them to bolster his own importance. The Prophet had paid Johnston a visit in Well's absence and the factor had not only believed his proclamations of friendship and non-aggression, but passed his opinion on to Eustis. This would prove embarrassing to Johnston as Harrison and Eustis were both increasingly aware that Well's information about the intentions of the Shawnee brothers was entirely accurate Johnston then reversed himself and suggested finding a way to be rid of the brothers. Johnston also weakened his case against Wells when he claimed that the officers of the fort, including Dr. Edwards, wanted the former agent removed, when in fact, they had testified for Wells.

Harrison arrived in Fort Wayne for another council in the fall of 1809. The sight of nearly fourteen hundred Indians encamped throughout the area must have caused some consternation on the part of Well's new bride. Even the children were unused to the clamor and commotion accompanying such a large congregation. Wells, although no longer agent, was concerned about keeping the Indians well fed. The Shawnee brothers and their followers were stirring up opposition to any further sale of land and William knew well how hunger could lead to violence. Although Little Turtle and Wells were also opposed to any more land cessions, they were caught in the middle between the militant Indians and the government land grabbers. Wells served as the official interpreter but his influence among the Miami was lessened by loss of his agency. Little Turtle, too, came under criticism for accepting government annuities. The Miami initially refused to comply with the Governor's request to sell more land. After much negotiation and the assurance that they would be compensated as the sole owners of the land in question, they acquiesced. The United States received 2.9 million acres of land at the treaty of Fort Wayne.

Many of the formerly loyal Miami were driven into Tecumseh's camp as a result of the treaty and it strengthened the resolve of the Shawnee leaders who were gathering their followers on the banks of the Tippecanoe River in Indiana on

the wrong side of the boundary line.
Wells re-visited the capital and lobbied for the reinstatement of his position during the winter of 1810-11. This time he had the backing of Senator John Pope and a number of influential Kentuckians. Eustis and Harrison were, above all, politicians, and were easily persuaded to make amends. Although Wells did not receive his agency back intact, he received appointment as sub agent for the Miami and Eel River tribes. Meanwhile, a frustrated Johnston resigned his post and was reassigned to Piqua, Ohio. Before leaving, he recommended another easterner, Benjamin Stickney, as his replacement.

Although Wells had won a partial triumph, his troubles were far from over. Impending war with Great Britain overshadowed any government interest in the civilization plan and Well's request that he be appointed supervisor of the plan was ignored. Tecumseh's influence was spreading rapidly and even the formerly loyal Miami were slipping over to the side of the militants. While Tecumseh traveled throughout the country gathering recruits, The Prophet resorted to murdering a number of outspoken dissidents, including Chief Leatherlips of the Wyandots. Harrison sent Wells to Prophetstown in April of 1811 to gather information on the killings. Tecumseh denied any part in the murders or depredations on the nearby settlements but confirmed his plan to stop white advances into former Indian territory at all costs. When Wells attempted to convince the Shawnee that his plan was doomed to failure, Tecumseh countered that the agent would indeed, live to see it succeed.

Wells delivered his report to Harrison and both men agreed that war was inevitable. Tecumseh and about three hundred followers traveled to Vincennes in July and confronted General Harrison with his intention to continue recruiting warriors from the south and to build a tribal federation to resist any future sale of lands to the United States. In a last attempt to settle their differences without force, Harrison directed Wells to a conference with the Miami on September 4. Little Turtle attended and assured the neutrality of his Miami but others indicated that they were ready to fight for their lands.

Harrison decided that the time for negotiations was over and began to make preparations for a march on Prophetstown. He sent out a request for volunteers and assembled an army of approximately one thousand men, composed of one third regular recruits and two thirds volunteers. Among the Kentuckians who responded were Major General Samuel Wells, in overall command of the Kentucky Mounted Rifles and William's new father-in-law, Colonel Frederick Geiger, leading one of the three militia units.

The Battle of Tippecanoe took place on November 7, 1811. The Americans encamped outside Prophetstown. On the afternoon of November 6, a small delegation approached the camp and asked for a parley with the Governor. The emissaries from both sides agreed to meet in council the next morning. However, before the council could convene, the Indians, incited by the Prophet, attacked the American camp shortly before dawn. Harrison had suspected such a move and had ordered his men to sleep fully clothed with weapons at their side. The first attack struck the areas where Samuel Wells and Frederick Geiger were encamped. Geiger was wounded but Samuel escaped unharmed to lead a successful counterattack. A second assault was also repulsed and after several unsuccessful rushes, the attackers fled the field. Both sides suffered casualties. Harrison's losses were by far the greatest but the Indians had been unusually vulnerable. It was later learned that the Prophet had promised that his magic power would protect them from American bullets and they neglected to use their usual caution when entering the American camp. It was a small victory for the Americans but the Prophet's reputation was damaged beyond repair. When Tecumseh returned in January of 1812, he banished his brother from any future involvement with the confederacy while he increased efforts to forge a tribal alliance. Meanwhile, Harrison again relied on Wells to deliver his speech to "each of the Miami tribes... in Indiana territory" in an attempt to bring the tribes into the American camp. [18]

The Tippecanoe incident increased Little Turtle's prestige among the Miami but his gout was becoming more disabling. He was unable to attend a meeting called by agent Stickney in April. However, when he learned that Tecumseh would address an assemblage of tribal leaders in Fort Wayne the following month, he made the effort to attend with the assistance of his son-in-law. He was rewarded by the steadfast opposition of the old chiefs plus the majority of the Miami and Delaware to Tecumseh's war plans.

Little Turtle, now gravely ill, made his last painful journey from Turtletown to the home of William Wells. His trip was ostensibly to obtain medical attention but he may also have wished to spend his last days at the site of old Kekionga, perhaps wistfully thinking of what might have been had his civilization plan succeeded. There was a certain drama surrounding this final visit as word of Little Turtle's condition spread and his old comrades and relatives began to gather in the orchard for the death vigil. The Wells children had grown accustomed to the assortment of Indian, Military and frontier people who passed through their father's home, but for twelve year old Polly, particularly, the procession must have been a curious sight. The news that war had finally been declared between the United States and Great Britain and the realization that Fort Wayne was vulnerable to invasion through Canada would contribute to the uneasiness of the moment.

Little Turtle remained in the home of his son-in-law for several weeks as talk centered around the impending war and Tecumseh's intentions. As his condition worsened, the Chief requested that he be carried into the orchard, where he died on July 14, 1812. Agent Stickney arranged a military funeral and the great warrior was accorded all the honors due a man of his stature. Even John Johnston, who had worked against him, had only laudatory comments after his death. William Wells and Little Turtle's relatives buried Mishikinakwa according to Miami ritual, with all his most valued possessions, including a dress sword presented by President Washington, eight silver medals, six pendants, twenty three silver crosses, his tomahawk, knives and several other utilitarian items. [19] Presumably, his other property, both real and personal, was distributed among his fellow tribesmen. William had described this custom many years earlier in his interview with Volney. Women, he pointed out, did not inherit the property of their husbands and at a warrior's death "not so much as their knives, or even pipes, descend to their children." A warrior, he explained, "caresses his children as any animal caresses its young," but when he leaves them to "go to war or the chace (sic)" he does not think of them anymore, and "exposes himself to danger, without caring what becomes of them." [20]

Wells was disgusted with government duplicity and the abandonment of the civilization plan and was concerned about the safety of his family at Fort Wayne. After Little Turtle's death he decided to cut his ties with Fort Wayne and move his family permanently to Louisville. Mary Geiger Wells, expecting her third child, may have exerted some pressure on her husband's decision. Letters between Anne and Rebecca imply that the comforts of Louisville held a greater attraction for their stepmother than the austere existence at Fort Wayne. Before Wells could resign, Harrison heard of his plans from Colonel Geiger and urged his agent to remain at his post and keep him informed of Indian activity. After insuring the safety of his family, Wells complied with Harrison's request.

The children and their stepmother and half brothers soon found themselves once again beholden to the hospitality of their Kentucky relatives. Samuel's commodious brick Georgian mansion on his 650 acre thoroughbred farm amply accommodated his extended family. [21] His own family was somewhat diminished in size as children married and scattered to distant places. Mary Wells Audrain likely remained at Fort Wayne. Rebecca and Nathan Heald had wed in 1810 and she had accompanied her husband to Fort Dearborn (Chicago) where he had accepted command. Margaret and Ann remained at home but Margaret would soon marry Jacob Geiger, brother of Mary Geiger Wells. Nevertheless, the close relationship between the cousins would continue. While the older girls were pre-occupied with "beaus," parties and gossip, Wayne and Polly were content to attend school and enjoy the usual pleasures of childhood. Their half-brothers, Samuel and Yelverton, were still toddlers and would accompany their mother when she moved into the Geiger household.

The Wells children bid good bye to their father, unaware that it would be their final farewell. They were well aware of his reputation as a fighter and as a man of bravery. The agent enjoyed relating tales of his earlier escapades and it was said that he could "entertain a company for hours" with his stories.[22]

He was often gone for long stretches of time and the children likely believed that he would, as usual, return home in a few weeks or even months, when his job was completed. Meanwhile, Fort Wayne, Fort Harrison (Indiana) and Fort Dearborn (Chicago) were in imminent danger of invasion. General William Hull, commander of the Army of the Northwest, ordered Heald to evacuate Fort Dearborn and march to Detroit (which Hull would surrender within days) or Fort Wayne, and urged Captain James Rhea, commander at Fort Wayne, to assist in the evacuation. While Rhea deliberated, Wells agreed to provide the escort for the retreating Americans. Well's decision was influenced by his desire to provide for the safety of Rebecca and her husband. He managed to assemble a small party of friendly Miami and accompanied by a military escort, they arrived at Fort Dearborn on August 13. The seriousness of the situation was immediately apparent. The number of Indians encamped around the fort was increasing daily and an air of militancy prevailed. Wells conferred with John Kinzie, an old acquaintance from Fort Wayne who operated a trading post at the settlement of Chicago. Together, they attempted to persuade Heald to make a stand and defend the fort but the young commander refused to disobey his orders. Meanwhile, Kinzie made preparations to evacuate his family by boat. Wells managed to convince the Indian leaders to convene a council to dissuade the warriors from their militant intentions and to insure the protection of the civilians, but the results were disheartening. The meeting only further convinced Wells that an attack on the retreating soldiers and civilians was inevitable. Nevertheless, on the morning of August 15, the garrison, including women and children and friendly Miami bravely marched through the gates of the fort. Rebecca Heald rode her own mare close to her husband's side. Her Uncle William, said to be in Indian dress and with his face blackened in anticipation of death, was in the lead. The women, children and remaining supplies followed in the wagons behind the regular soldiers and the militia. They proceeded for about a mile and a half when Wells spotted a group of Pottawatomies forming an ambush behind the dunes. He shouted a warning but the enemy was already upon them. The less than one hundred Americans were overwhelmed by over four hundred hostile warriors. While Heald and Wells massed a charge, bands of Indians reached the wagons and slaughtered many of the women and children, including Rebecca's devoted slave, Cicely, who had been with her since childhood and accompanied her to the frontier, and Cecily's infant child. Wells rode toward Rebecca but was hit several times. He continued to fight until he was struck again and pinned beneath his horse. As his niece watched in horror, his attackers decapitated him and cut out his heart and devoured it. This was a ritual reserved for those who were greatly admired and whose courage the Indians hoped to gain. With the death of Little Turtle and now, William Wells, the "civilization plan" was doomed.

Three fourths of the little procession that left Fort Dearborn were dead and most of the remainder were taken captive. Rebecca survived six gunshot wounds but in spite of her heroic efforts to save herself, was finally captured. Due to the intervention of John Kinzie, she was purchased from her captor by Kinzie's employee, Chardonaise, a half breed Indian, for a mule and a quart of whiskey. Captain Heald, seriously wounded in the hip, also ended up in the protection of Kenzie and his loyal employees and friendly Indians. They were taken to Fort Mackinaw where they surrendered to the British and after a circuitous journey by canoe, ultimately arrived in Detroit, which had also fallen to the British. Heald was later paroled to Pittsburgh where he wrote his official report of the massacre. While the Healds were making their way toward home, Samuel Wells, accompanied by three of his sons, led his Kentucky Mounted Unit under command of General Harrison to relieve Fort Wayne, which had been besieged since the fall of Fort Dearborn. Colonel Geiger also joined the relief expedition which arrived shortly after the departure of the warriors. The civilians, which may have included Mary Wells Audrain, had taken refuge in the fort. Her husband, James Audrain, who served in Harrison's Army of the Northwest joined Wells at this time. He accompanied the Seventeenth Infantry under command of his father in law to the foot of rapids of the Maumee River where Wells was ordered to begin construction of a fortification. Meanwhile, in January, General James Winchester, after establishing a position at the rapids of the Maumee River was informed that food and supplies for his troops were available at Frenchtown (Monroe, Michigan) and that the settlement was unsecured. In an ill advised move, he took his troops, including two companies of the Seventeenth, to march on to the French settlement but he neglected to fortify their position. A large force of British, Wyandot and Ottawa attacked on January 22, burned the buildings with wounded inside and took the able survivors captive. William's nephew, Levi Wells was among those killed.

The terrible details of William Well's heroic and tragic death were brought to Fort Wayne by Miami warrior who had managed to escape and the message eventually found its way to Louisville. Although Well's widow surely recognized the dangers facing her husband, the manner of his death would be received with shock and horror by the entire family. In addition, no word of the whereabouts of Rebecca and Nathan had been received. Some sources claim that a family friend, Colonel O'Fallen, formerly of Louisville, came across some personal articles, including a jewelry trunk belonging to Rebecca, in the possession of an Indian woman. O'Fallen purchased them and sent them on to her father, causing the family to believe that the young couple had been killed in the massacre. Thus, it was a joyous reunion when the Healds finally arrived in Louisville in the fall of 1816 and were reunited with Rebecca's family. William Well's daughter Rebecca was away at school and missed the reunion but urged her sister, Anne to sent her "all the particulars of their narrow escape!" [23]

William Wells in military uniform,
probably between 1805 and 1810.
Chicago Historical Society.

Chief Little Turtle.
Reproduction. Courtesy Lucas County/Maumee Valley Historical Society.
Original painting is owned by Indiana Historical Society

REBEKAH HEALD.

Rebecca Wells Heald,
daughter of Samuel Wells.
Center For Archival Collections,
Bowling Green, Ohio.

Signing of the Treaty of Greenville by Howard Christy Chandler. Little Turtle is addressing General Anthony Wayne. William Wells is standing in center.
Copy, LC/MVHS.

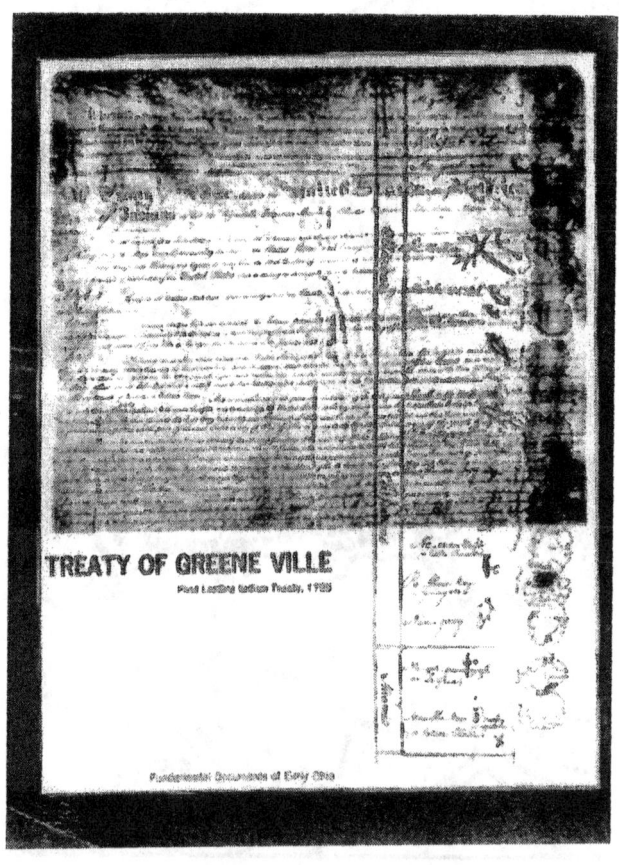

Treaty of Greenville,
Little Turtle's signature in right corner.
Ohio Historical Society.

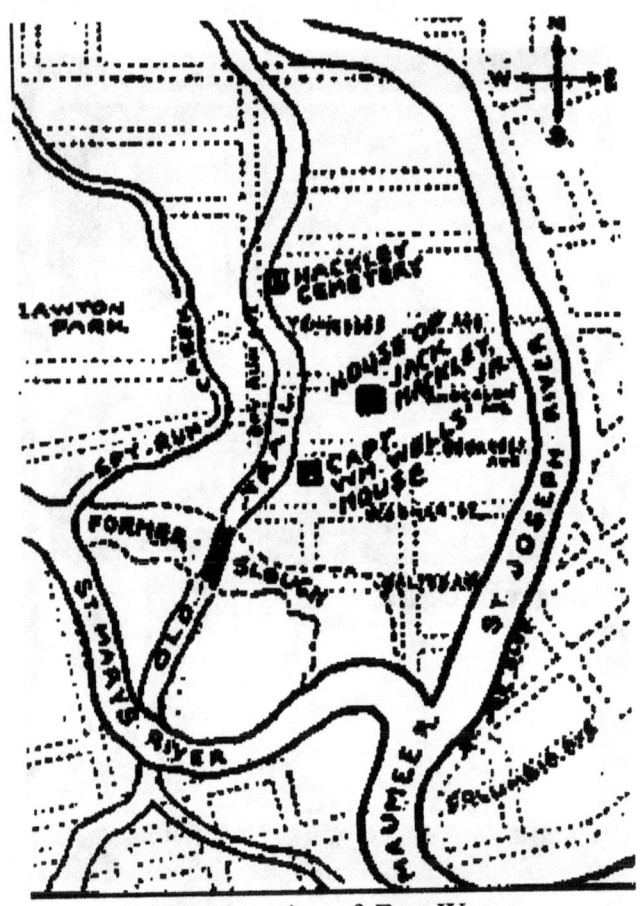

Map of portion of Fort Wayne showing Well's pre-emption.
Griswold, Pictorial History of Fort Wayne.

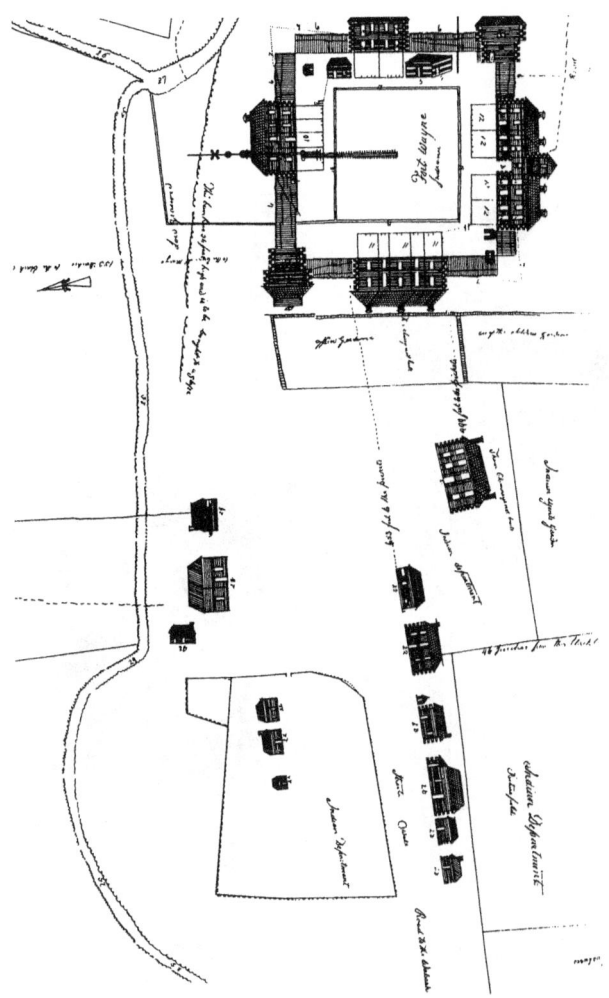

Map of Fort Wayne showing garrison and auxiliary buildings
Original drawn by Major John Whistler in National Archives. Copy redrawn by Michael R. Ormiston, 1983. Fort Wayne Historical Society.

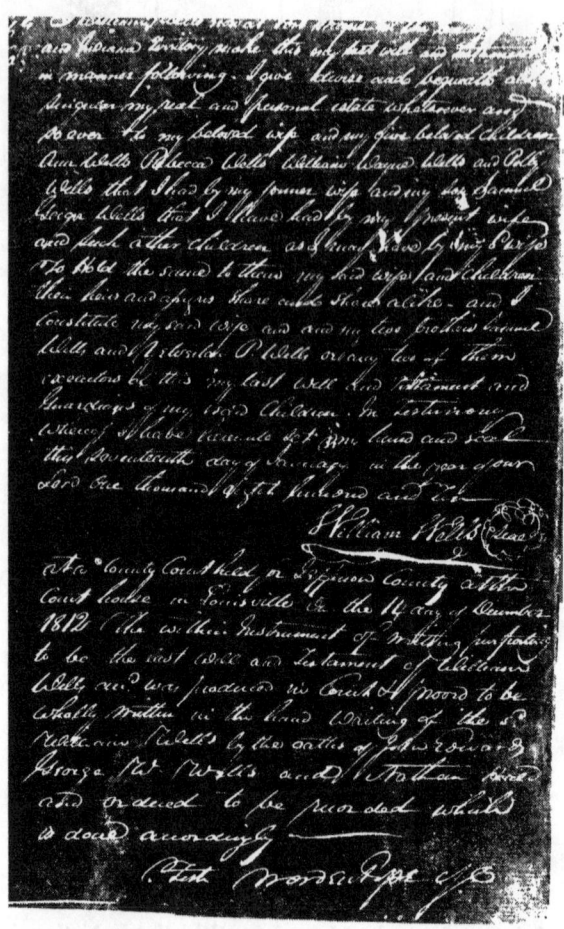

Portion of Well's will containing his signature.
Copy, LC/MVHS, Allen County Historical Society

STATE OF KENTUCKY, Jefferson circuit, sct. October term, 1827, 12th November: Robert Turner and Mary his wife, executors of William Wells, deceased, complainants against Ann Turner, Rebecca Hackley, James Walcott and Polly his wife, William W. Wells, Samuel G. Wells, Yelverton P. Wells, Juliann Wells, children and devisees of the said William Wells, deceased, defendants in chancery. This day came the complainants by their counsel, and it appearing to the satisfaction of the court, that the defendants Ann Turner, Rebecca Hackley and James Walcott and Polly his wife and W. W. Wells, are non-residents of this commonwealth, and they not having appeared and answered the said complainants bill; it is therefore ordered, that they appear here on or before the tenth day of the next January term of this court, and answer the said complainants bill, otherwise the same will be taken for confessed, as to and against them, and the matter thereof decreed accordingly; and it is further ordered, that a copy of this order be published two months successively, in some public authorized newspaper of this State. A copy test,

WORDEN POPE, *Clerk.*

nov 17—951m2w By JOHN W. TYLER, D. C.

Notice of suit filed by Robert and Mary Turner against Well's heirs. Kentucky newspaper clipping, 1827. Copy, LC/MVHS

A typical two story log house, c. 1818 in Fort Wayne is similar to descriptions of William Well's home in Wellsington.

Little Turtle's gravesite in Fort Wayne. The plaque reads in part:
" Chief of the Miami Indians
Teacher of his people
Friend of the United States
His endeavors toward peace should serve as an inspiration for future generations...."

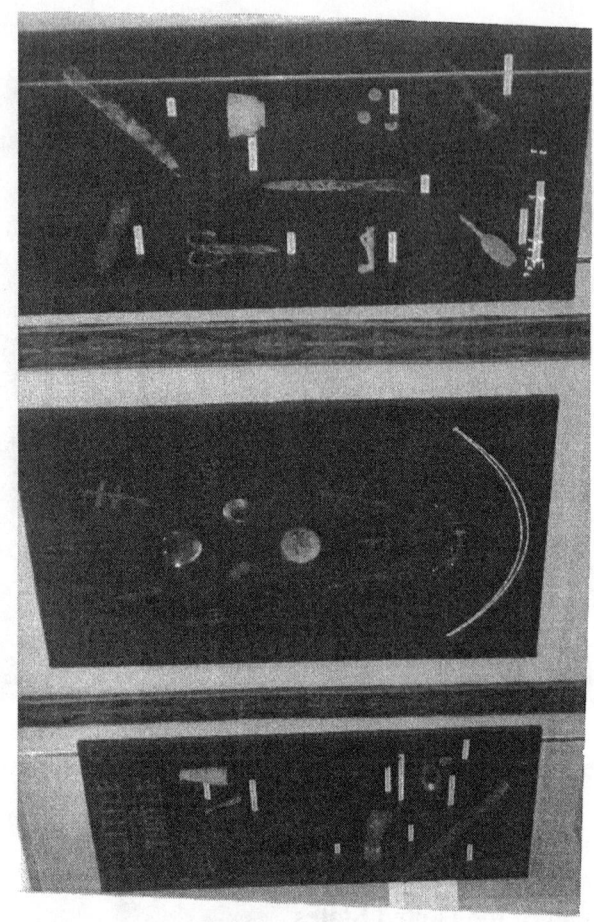

Articles once buried with Little Turtle are on display at the Indiana Historical Society, Indianapolis, Indiana.

Chapter II
Mary Wells and Her Sisters

After the death of William Wells, life returned to normal for his children, who remained with their uncle in Louisville. Wayne attended a private school to prepare for an appointment to West Point. Samuel Wells appears to have had a genuine affection and interest in the welfare and happiness of his brother's children. In a letter to his niece, Rebecca, he expressed his concern for the future of William Wayne and his hope that he would attend the military academy "for a few years at lest (sic)..." If he found that he did not care for that profession, it was Samuel's "earnest wish for him to try business." Seventeen year old Rebecca was attending boarding school in Lexington. She confided in her sister, Anne, that she was lonely, but was learning "Spelling, Reading, Writing, and shortly (would) begin Geography." These "are the sciences," she wrote, "that our dear deceased Father wished for me to learn." Only Anne seemed anxious to return to Wellsington and her homesickness may have had more to do with a young doctor she met in Fort Wayne than a desire to leave the comfort of her uncle's home.

The older Wells girls, in fact, were eligible young women of marriageable age. It was well known that Wells left a considerable estate, including 1,200 acres at Piqua, Ohio and the preemption rights to 320 acres at Fort Wayne. Included in his will are six black slaves and their children and two indentured servants. He also owned considerable personal property including four horses, invaluable assets on the frontier. Some estimates list his estate as about nine thousand dollars, a considerable sum for that time. [24] Well's will, written in 1810, specified that his estate be divided among his "beloved wife," Mary Geiger Wells and his "beloved" children, Anne Wells, Rebecca Wells, William Wayne Wells and Polly (Mary) Wells, that he had by Sweet Breeze, and Samuel Geiger Wells with provisions for "any other children" as he might have by his present wife. Mary Geiger Wells was named as executrix of the estate and Well's brothers, Samuel and Yelverton were to share guardianship of the children with Mrs. Wells.

The children of William and Sweet Breeze were also in line to receive generous land grants from any future treaties which the United States government might enter into with the Miami Nation. Thus, suitably educated, schooled in the social graces and with respectable dowries, the Wells girls would attract many "beaus." One such prospective suitor was Dr. William Turner. The doctor had served as surgeon for the Fort Wayne garrison since 1810 and was well acquainted with the Wells sisters and their prospects. Turner continued to court Anne in Louisville and frequently visited the girls. During the winter of 1812, Rebecca requested that he bring her "great coat" which she had left behind, if he intended on "coming to Lexington soon."[25] Although promoted in 1813, Turner resigned his commission that same year and embarked on a campaign to receive an appointment as government Indian agent, a post then held by Benjamin Stickney. He was more successful in his pursuit of Anne and after their marriage in Louisville in 1815, the couple returned to Wellsington. In 1817, possibly in a move to enhance his qualifications, Turner compiled "A Description of the Emigration, Habits, etc. of the Northwestern Indians" for "his friend," Major Francis S. Bretton of Detroit.

Rebecca completed her schooling and returned to be with her sister at Wellsington. Soon after, Anne and Rebecca's half sister, Jane, was also taken into the Turner household. In a later correspondence, Anne writes that when her husband was questioned if Jane "was not Papa's child," the Doctor answered in the affirmative, adding that he had taken "Jane from a state of want as his own child." Wayne also spent time with his sisters before going on to West Point. Only Polly (Mary) was missing from the family circle at Fort Wayne.

There was little to attract a young girl to Fort Wayne at that time. Primarily a military outpost, Indian Agency and trading post, whose major purpose for existence was the annual distribution of government annuities to the Indians, Fort Wayne was devoid of cultural refinement. The few women in residence were wives of military personnel or agents and traders. The French families congregated at Frenchtown while most of the Americans lived in the safety of the garrison or within its shadow on the opposite side of the St. Marys River from Wellsington. Anne's letters paint a dismal picture of the manners and morale of the military. Instead of providing protection for the civilians, Anne writes that "neither the lives or property of the citizens were secure" and reveals that several citizens had been waylaid by soldiers, presumably drunk and disorderly, between the garrison and Frenchtown,. Specifically, Francis Audrain and a number more on this side of the river, " between the Doctor's shop and the garden at Wellsington." As a precautionary measure, Dr. Turner employed several members of the Miami to guard the estate. Although Anne and Rebecca appear to view the military with disdain, they had several friends among the Americans. They seem especially fond of the families of William Oliver, a hero of the siege of Fort Meigs and now a government trader and land speculator, and his brother, Peter, also a trader. "Mrs. Oliver" was a "fine neighbor" and "Miss Oliver" was a "great deal of company." Miss Oliver was about to be married to Francis Audrain and Anne was quite complimentary in her description of Miss Oliver's wedding dress, a "handsome muslim robe." Anne also mentions Mrs. Clark, wife of Lieutenant Clark, as a "charming companion, " but makes no reference to the wife and daughter of Agent Benjamin Stickney, for whom the government provided a new log house. The Reverend Isaac McCoy and his family also resided at Fort Wayne during this period and Anne and Rebecca regularly attended meetings at the Baptist mission.

While Anne and Rebecca were residing at Wellsington, several of their mother's relatives were living in Miami villages near Fort Wayne. Their cousin, Kilsoquah, referred to as the "beloved granddaughter" of Little Turtle although she was born only two years before his death, spent her childhood years near Roanoke, Indiana on a 320 acre section of land granted to her father, Makeshenequah (or Wakshingay), a son of the great chieftain. During a brief marriage to John Owl, she lived near her grandfather's home at Turtletown. After her husband's death, she returned to Roanoke, married Anthony Revarre and four children were born to them. Both of Kilsoquah's husbands were of French and Indian descent. None of Little Turtle's granddaughters appear to have married full blooded Miami but all would be provided for in government treaties. Kilsoquah was well known throughout the Indian and white community and her home near Roanoke was a point of interest for tourists as late as 1941. At Kilsoquah's death in 1915 at the age of 105, according to some sources, she was said to be the only full blooded Indian in Huntington County. Another cousin, Coesse, son of Makkatamonquah (or Katemongwah), the other son of Little Turtle, was chief of his own village near Turtletown. Before he and his family moved to the Miami settlement near Peru, they lived on land south of Columbia City, granted earlier to his father.

 The Wells children (with the exception of Polly) lived most of their lives within twenty five miles of each other but there is no record of any contact between the families and no indication that they were aware of each others existence. It was said that Kilsoquah never learned the English language and spoke only through an interpreter, usually her son, Anthony. Perhaps this was passed on from her grandfather who occasionally found it to his advantage to depend on Wells to interpret the speech of the Americans. Conversely, the Wells children were schooled in English at an early age and being constantly surrounded by English speaking people, may have forgotten any Miami words or phrases they learned from their mother.

Anne and Rebecca chose to return to Fort Wayne but they remained close to their Kentucky cousins and corresponded regularly. The letters of Ann F. Wells are full of gossip about her Louisville neighbors. Ann inquired of Rebecca as to "how many baus (sic)" she had and added that an old friend, Captain James Hackley, then stationed at Fort Dearborn, was heading to the "civilized world" to find a wife. "You must set your cap for him," she advised. Rebecca took her cousin's advice and shortly after Captain Hackley arrived in Fort Wayne she accepted his proposal, prompting her Uncle Samuel who had served with him in the late war, to send his blessing. He is "one of my best young friends" he counseled, and a "lovely man." The couple were married in the spring and Rebecca embarked upon the nomadic life of an army wife .
Throughout this period, Polly remained in Louisville where another wedding was creating great interest. As early as December, 1816, Ann had written Rebecca that William's widow (Rebecca's stepmother) , Mary Geiger Wells, was daily awaiting the arrival of Mr. Robert Turner, who she was engaged to marry. It was quite acceptable for a woman of Mrs. Well's youth with young children to care for, to remarry within a suitable period of time. Ann did not speculate how young Polly felt about the upcoming marriage, but announced that she and others were planning to "have a great piece of fun at the wedding." The marriage would take place on May 8, 1817 but none of Mrs. Well's stepdaughters would be in attendance. In the meantime, the young ladies and matrons of Louisville were all preparing for the winter midtown balls. Ann mentions a "masonic ball" to be held within the next few days. At sixteen, Mary Polly was presumably of an eligible age to attend the many gatherings of the busy Louisville social season, but Ann notes only that she and her aunt planned to attend the ball.

Not all family members were pleased about the impending

marriage of Mrs. Wells and Mr. Turner. Although Robert and Anne's husband, William, were brothers, the Doctor was threatened by loss of control of Well's estate. Both William Turner and Mrs. Well's brother, Jacob Geiger, had advised Mrs. Wells on financial matters since her husband's death but that would quickly change. Shortly after the wedding, Robert wrote to his brother that he was now in charge of the estate. Moreover, he claimed to have found that Well's children by Sweet Breeze had received "from 150 to 200 dollars more in money than they were entitled to" and consequently, a recent draft to William Turner & Co. could not be paid. Dr. Turner expressed his concern in a letter to Rebecca and suggested that he and Captain Hackley must take immediate steps "to see that justice is extended to all parties." The situation continued to deteriorate. Robert Turner and Jacob Geiger argued over the settlement of the estate and Geiger accused his sister of being a "mischief maker" and a "false tale bearer." Colonel Geiger was also present and accused Jacob of defrauding the estate. The disposition of William Well's estate and any future distribution of property or government lands would continue to cause dissent within the family.

  William Turner continued to press for government appointments for himself. In 1817, he attended a treaty signing at the mouth of the Maumee River. For some time, talk in Fort Wayne had centered around the possibility of a canal connecting Lake Erie, the Foot of the Rapids of the lower Maumee and Fort Wayne. Benjamin Stickney was among the most visionary of the canal promoters. When the Treaty of 1817 opened up the lands on the lower Maumee, Stickney and Major William Oliver were among the major purchasers. Stickney proceeded to lay out a town site which he christened Vistula. Oliver, as agent for the Martin Baum Company, purchased lands at a site later known as Port Lawrence and an up river site at the entrance of the twelve mile square at the Foot of the Rapids of the Maumee River. He oversaw the platting of what would become the town of Maumee City and directed the construction of the Central House, a hotel for travelers and prospective investors. William Turner did not purchase lands but he surely must have been interested in the prospects. Several years later, Polly and her husband, James Wolcott would reside briefly in this same hotel before building their new home downriver.

Meanwhile, Anne Turner, expecting her first child, often found herself alone in Fort Wayne. Dr. Turner made frequent trips to the capitol at Vincennes and was absent for days at a time. Rebecca had accompanied her husband to his post at Fort Dearborn and later to Greenbay, Wisconsin where her daughter, Ann, named for her sister, was born in 1818. Both the Peter Oliver and William Oliver families were making preparations to move to the Foot of the Rapids. Even the family of Benjamin was leaving for the lower Maumee, providing an opportunity for Turner to lobby more vigorously for Stickney's position. Miss Oliver remained and stayed with Anne through her "confinement" and the birth of the Turner's daughter, Maria Louisa. Anne found much pleasure in her new daughter and younger half sister and occupied her time in sewing and needlework, but she missed her sister's company. She continued to encourage Rebecca to pressure Captain Hackley to transfer closer to Fort Wayne.

Anne's loneliness was compounded when she learned that her "nearly infant" youngest sister, Polly, was moving further west and she feared she might never see her again. As early as the fall of 1816, cousin Ann Wells had revealed that her father was planning to join the great migration into Missouri and would be taking his family, including Polly Wells, with him.

Years earlier, before the United States acquired the Louisiana Purchase in 1803, another Kentuckian, Daniel Boone, left Kentucky in search of more "elbow room" and settled in present day, St. Charles County, Missouri. By 1812, Missouri had become a territory and Boone's former neighbors from Kentucky and Virginia were pouring into the area around St. Louis. Missouri was particularly attractive to southerners as slavery was not only legal but commonplace and pressure was being exerted on Congress to admit the territory as a slave state. Samuel's daughter Mary and her husband, James Audrain settled in St. Charles County as early as 1816. By February of the following year, Samuel confirmed to his niece, Rebecca, that the family was definitely planning to join a large group of relatives and neighbors, including slaves, servants and livestock leaving the next month for St. Charles. Daughter, Rebecca and her husband Nathan Heald would accompany them, as would Samuel's sons, George and Samuel, Jr. and their families. Included in the family group would be Polly (Mary) Wells, who Samuel noted was well and "sends her love to you" and to her brother, William Wayne. Samuel encourages Rebecca to also "join us on the Missoury (sic) it is much better cuntry (sic) to live in then where you are and you will be among your friends."

The group of approximately sixty Kentuckians set off for Missouri territory on March 20, 1817. They departed by flatboat down the Ohio River to the Mississippi and headed for the Missouri River. Some of their livestock would be loaded onto a separate boat and the remainder would be driven overland. Staying behind was Samuel's daughter, Margaret Wells Geiger and her newborn son. She confessed to Rebecca that she was "distressed beyond anything that I could have expected." Margaret lamented that her small family and that of her Uncle Yelverton were all that was left of "once a large and growing family."

Anne and Rebecca were equally as distressed as their cousin Margaret over the departure of their younger sister to the Missouri frontier. There is no record of any correspondence from Polly to her sisters, defending her decision to leave but Anne informed Rebecca in the spring of 1817 that there were several letters from Kentucky awaiting her in Fort Wayne which contain, "no doubt, the unpleasant and melancholy intelligence of our...sister's departure." This information, she continued, was of the "most disturbing kind." Anne does not seem to have shared the close bonds established between her sisters and her uncle and she appears to be estranged from her stepmother. She writes that if Polly had "gone with persons in whom I had the least rays of glimmering confidence" she would have been less distraught and she urges Rebecca to enlist their stepmother's assistance in persuading their sister to come to Fort Wayne. She also notes that Wayne, who was very attached to his sister Polly was "very sorry" at her departure. Wayne, in his own letter expressed his astonishment "that Mamma should consent to let her go."

In addition to her concern over the departure of her youngest sister, other matters weighed heavily on Anne's mind. Early in 1818, Anne confided in Rebecca that "we (the Turners) are living extravagantly as usual" and "without any visible income." This situation would soon improve. On October 6, 1818, United States Commissioners, Jonathan Jennings, Lewis Cass and Benjamin Park met with representatives of the Miami Nation to negotiate a treaty. Known as the Treaty of St. Marys, this treaty included several grants of land to the Wells children. Ann Wells Turner, William Wayne Wells, Mary Wells, Jane Turner Wells and Rebecca Wells Hackly, each a "half blooded Indian" were awarded individually, one section of land "by patent, in fee simple." Dr. Turner had managed to procure appointment as secretary to this commission. Among those present at the treaty signing were Indian agents Benjamin Stickney and Well's old nemesis, John Johnston and sub agents John Kenzie, Gabriel Godfroy and William Oliver. Soon after, Dr. Turner succeeded in obtaining an appointment as Indian agent for the Miami and would assume all of Stickney's duties within the next two years.

Anne's happiness was almost complete when her sister,

Rebecca, returned to Wellsington with her family and settled on a nearby farm on Well's preemption land. James Hackley, perhaps influenced by his wife's new status as landowner, had resigned his commission. Although life as an officer in the military could provide a reasonable standard of living, Hackley no doubt envisioned the prosperity that could come when the lands would become available to the public.

Re-united, the sisters intensified their efforts to bring Polly to Wellsington. Anne had earlier expressed confidence that "should she not be married, which Heaven forbid," Polly would eventually consent to live with one of them. Anne pleaded with Nathan Heald to do "everything in his power," and wrote to Polly and her Uncle Samuel in hopes of persuading her to leave. Their stepmother finally agreed to send for her if she were willing but Polly, now nearly eighteen and known as Mary, as befitted her age, appeared to be quite content with her uncle's family and chose to remain with them in St. Charles.

The World of Mary Wells Wolcott

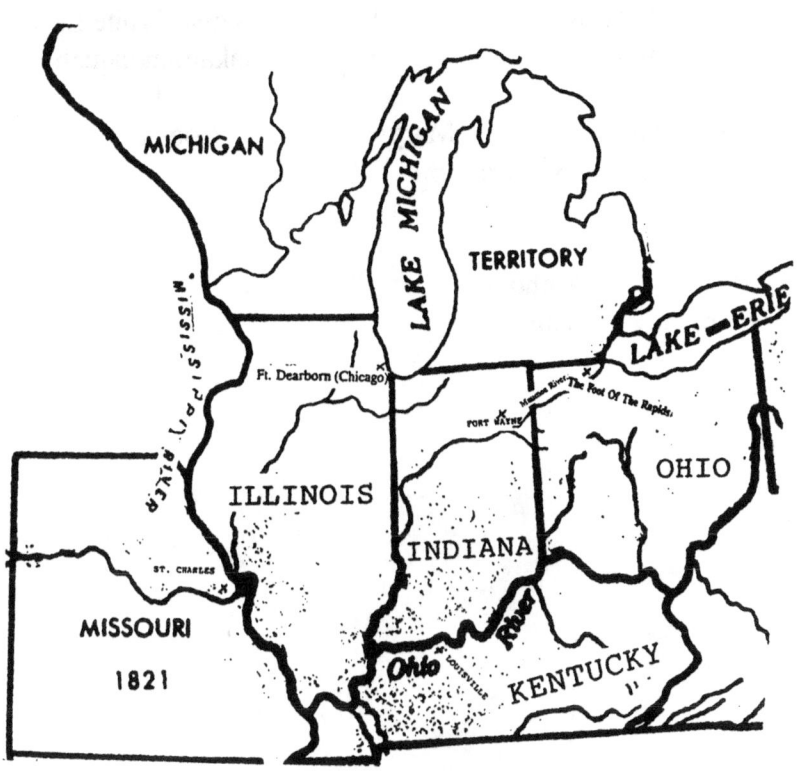

Mary Well's Maternal Cousins

```
                        Little Turtle
                             |
                        Sweet Breeze
 Makeshenquah                |            Great White Loon
 (Wakshingay)                |            (Makattamonquah)
      |                                          |
   Kilsoquah              Mary                 Coesse
 m. Anthony Rivarre
      |         |
    Mary     Anthony
 . m Guy Froman
```

Family of William Wells

Samuel Wells, Sr. and Elizabeth Hayden Wells
|
William Wells (Sweet Breeze)
|
Ann Wells c.1793-1834   (William Turner)
Rebecca Wells 1795-1835   (James Hackley)
William Wayne 1797-1832
Mary (Polly) 1800-1843   (James Wolcott)

       (Mary Geiger)
Samuel 1810
Julianna ?
Yelverton 1812

       (Unknown)
Jane   1808 - ? Jane and John Griggs celebrated their
          Golden Wedding in 1880.

Children of Samuel Wells, Jr. and Mary Spears
   Margaret 1783 (Jacob Geiger)
   Mary   1785   (James Audrain)
   Samuel 1788
   Rebecca 1790 (Nathan Heald)
   Levi 1792
   George W. 1794
   Ann F. 1799

Home of Samuel Wells in Louisville where Mary Wells spent her youth. Wells purchased the land in 1805. Courtesy, Hon. Maria Kitty Mueter, p.109.

Chapter III

James and Mary Wolcott

A Connecticut Yankee and Little Turtle's Granddaughter

    St. Louis was a bustling frontier town in 1820 and a key point in western expansion. Neighboring St. Charles County was no longer the isolated territory which had attracted Daniel Boone. The hunter/trader was replaced by large organized groups such as that of the Wells family. Scores of travelers, entrepreneurs and new settlers hoping to re-establish the homes and farms they left behind, passed through the portals of St. Charles on the Missouri River. Among those attracted to the Missouri Territory was thirty-one year old James Wolcott, a Connecticut "Yankee" who hoped to find his fortune in the West.
    James was one of thirteen children born to Guy and Abigail Wolcott, members of a prominent Connecticut family which included two former governors and a signer of the Declaration of Independence. As James reached manhood, the Connecticut economy was still suffering from the effects of war time deprivations and an expanding population. James left his home in Torrington to work in a woolen mill in nearby Middletown. It was here that he likely met James M. Riley, a man well acquainted with members of the Wolcott family. While James was working in Middletown, the United States was once again drifting toward war with England, an act which would cut off the flow of European textiles. James, recognizing the opportunity for expansion of the domestic market, returned to Torrington and convinced his Uncle Frederick Wolcott to finance the construction of a woolen mill The mill opened in 1813 at a site which later became known as Wolcottville. As James had hoped, the business flourished during the war years. However, during the post war period

the textile trade again opened to competition and the domestic textile industry experienced a temporary recession. The mill was mortgaged to Governor Oliver Wolcott in 1816 although Guy, Sr. and several relatives continued to own property in Wolcottville. Meanwhile, thousands of residents were leaving New England for the new West. Connecticut had retained land in the Western Reserve of northeast Ohio and the Firelands had been reserved for those who had lost property at the hands of the British during the Revolutionary War. The Connecticut Land Company was busy laying out townsites and selling farm plots. James's younger brother, Guy, had already left for "New Connecticut and by 1817, had purchased several farms near Stowe and Tallmadge. Guy, Sr. and Abigail and several of their children joined the migration. The following year, James, with a letter of recommendation for Joseph F. Hughes, a newspaperman and town promoter in Delaware, Ohio, set off for the West.

During his two year residency, James supervised the construction and operation of a woolen mill for Mr. Hughes. It was while living in Delaware that James became acquainted with the Episcopal Church and he converted from the traditional Congregational faith of his ancestors in 1819. This relationship would prove beneficial to both parties. It was also while in Delaware that James presumably heard of opportunities opening further west. An acquaintance, Milo Pettibone, a Delaware lawyer, had a cousin who practiced law in the rapidly growing city of St. Louis. Pettibone provided James with a letter of introduction to his cousin in which he refers to Wolcott as "a gentleman whose character stands perfectly fair here and who is very much respected." Wolcott, according to Pettibone's letter had a "reputation as quite a mechanical genius" and was interested in "embarking on almost any business of a mechanical nature."[26] Thus, armed with Pettibone's letter of approval, Wolcott left for Missouri in March of 1820. Almost exactly one year later, James Wolcott and Mary Wells were married in St. Charles County, Missouri. How the paths of a Connecticut Yankee in search of "mechanical work" and the granddaughter of the great Chief Little Turtle came to cross remains a cause for speculation. Several coincidences may have thrown them together. Mary's cousins, Rebecca and Nathan Heald were well acquainted with the John Kenzie family dating from their tragic experience at Fort Dearborn. Dr. Alexander Wolcott, James Wolcott's first cousin, met and married a sister of John Kenzie while serving as Indian Agent at Fort Dearborn in 1820. Letters of introduction between the two families could have brought the young couple together. A more plausible explanation may be that upon arrival in St. Louis, James was directed to St. Charles by an acquaintance of James Audrain, Samuel Well's son-in-law. Audrain built a mill on the Peruque Creek sometime after 1817 and may have hired Wolcott to superintend his operations. Frontier society was small and eligible young men and women of marriageable age were few. Thus, it was not uncommon for friends to play the part of matchmaker. Moreover, by frontier standards, it was none too soon for twenty-one year old Mary Wells and James Wolcott, ten years her senior, to be finding suitable mates. Their marriage on March 9, 1821 was evidently blessed by family and friends as witnessed by the signatures of Samuel Wells, Nathan Heald and James Audrain on the official certificate. The service was performed by an "ordained minister," although it presumably took place in the home of Samuel Wells, or possibly Rebecca and Nathan Heald, as a church had yet to be built in St. Charles County. Frontier weddings provided one of the few social affairs attended by family and neighbors and the celebration often lasted well into the night or the following day. The marriage of James and Mary was likely no exception and although there were no members of the bride's immediate family present, her cousins, Rebecca Heald and Mary Audrain were there to attend her.

The whereabouts of the Wolcotts following their marriage is unclear. Some sources maintain that the young couple moved to Fort Wayne where James served as associate judge of the common pleas court. Evidence does not bear this theory out. Allen county was not formed until 1823 and Fort Wayne did not become the Seat of Justice until the following year. Moreover, James Wolcott's name is not included in the list of first associate judges of Allen or Randolph Counties. If William Wells Wolcott is to be believed, his parents returned to Louisville within the first year as he gives Kentucky as his birthplace in 1821.. The newlyweds could, however, have visited briefly near Wellsington to renew family ties with Mary's sisters. If so, this would be their first reunion in over five years and much had taken place in that interval.

The Treaty of 1818 had improved the financial fortunes of William Well's children but personal doubts and tragedies continued to plague them. Anne's letters to Rebecca had long demonstrated a melancholy preoccupation with her "destiny" and she requested her sister to promise to care for their half sister, Jane, in case of her own premature death. It was not because of any lack of "confidence" in her husband, she explained, but because she felt blood ties were stronger. Her letters indicate a growing dissatisfaction with her husband's frequent absences. Married women had few rights over the control of their property or finances and Turner was often gone for long periods while attending to his wife's financial affairs as well as his own. In addition, Turner and his brother-in-law, James Hackley, were said to take advantage of the tribal rights of their wives. Indian Agent, John Hay, apparently referring to services provided to the Miami, complained that they (Turner and Hackley) are "Indians when interested and Whites when not."[27] Like so many men on the frontier, both men were said to be heavy drinkers. Turner's heavy drinking may be what prompted Anne to confide in Rebecca that she sometimes felt "half deranged" from worry and cautioned her sister to "guess not at my apparent cause of unhappiness, I sometimes think I let it pray (sic) too heavily on my mind. ..." promising "I will tell you all" when they next met. By 1820, Turner was relieved of his position as Indian Agent. The official cause was "unsatisfactory conduct" but Turner's investment of government annuities in a failed Cincinnati bank likely contributed to his dismissal. The doctor's drinking was exacerbated by his deteriorating health and the couple appear to have separated by 1821.[28] All mention of the Turner's daughter, Maria Louisa also disappears and she is not referred to again until 1833 when Anne sent "a ring with the hair of my only child who I hope, is in heaven" to her niece and namesake, Ann T. Hackley.. Rebecca's situation appeared more stable. Daughter Ann was quickly followed by son, Jack, and another daughter, Elizabeth was born in 1820. Elizabeth's health was precarious and she would live only three years. Thus, if James and Mary resided briefly in Fort Wayne, it was in the midst of an uneasy time for the Wells family.

It was however, a time of growth for Fort Wayne and the surrounding area. As subsequent treaties acquired more land from the Indian tribes for government sale, speculators, town builders and traders swarmed into western Ohio and eastern Indiana. Anthony Shane, old comrade of William Wells, laid out a town plat on the Ohio-Indiana border on the reservation granted to him by the federal government for his services in the Indian wars. Among the investors in his town lots was James Hackley. Shanesville was one of many town sites to spring up along the St. Marys River. Nearby was the town of Willshire, platted by Captain James Riley, the Wolcott family friend from Middletown, Connecticut. Riley had come west several years earlier to survey government lands. He founded Willshire in western Ohio in 1821.[29] While still serving as a surveyor, Riley often traveled between Willshire and Fort Wayne. Although separated by forty miles of wilderness, water traffic on the St. Mary River between the two communities was relatively

heavy. While in Fort Wayne, Riley made the acquaintance of James Hackley and William Turner. Hackley was one of the founders and served as treasurer of the Masonic Lodge in Fort Wayne where Riley, also a mason, likely attended. It may have been Hackley who brought the two former neighbors, James Wolcott and James Riley together. Riley was familiar with Wolcott's experience in building and superintending mills and he hired him to run his new mill in Willshire. Wolcott purchased land in Willshire in 1823 and built a frame home for his family, which by then included two
year old William Wells and baby, Robert Fulton. Wolcott shared Riley's hope that Willshire would prove to be a center of commerce and he served in several civic capacities, including Recorder of Deeds in 1824 and Associate Judge of Mercer County Common Pleas Court at Shanesville in 1825 and 1826. Little is known of Mary's activities in Willshire but Riley's son, William W. Riley, later referred to her as "an educated young lady." He also indicates that the youngest Wells daughter, "about 16 in 1826 " lived with "Mrs. Walcott in Willshire " [30] This would likely be Jane Wells Turner who would be about fourteen years old at that time.

    James Riley and James Wolcott, in addition to their economic aspirations, shared a lively interest in politics. Both were admirers of Henry Clay. The former Kentucky Senator and presidential candidate was a personal friend of Riley and made at least one visit to Wilshire en route to Fort Wayne in 1824. He was accompanied by Wolcott's brother-in-law, James Hackley and General John Tipton, then Indian Agent at Fort Wayne. James Wolcott was almost certainly included in the group which gathered around Mr. Clay to applaud and endorse his political doctrines. Wolcott's esteem is evidenced in the choice of name for his third son, Henry Clay Wolcott, born in 1830. Wolcott's interest in politics would continue throughout much of his life and was later shared by his son, James Monroe Wolcott, named in honor of the former president.

By 1825, ground was broken for the Ohio and Erie Canal and entrepreneurial interest shifted to the lower Maumee Valley where another canal was projected to link Lake Erie with Indiana. The town sites earlier laid out by Benjamin Stickney at Vistula and William Oliver at Port Lawrence and the Foot of the Rapids (Maumee) on the lower Maumee River were already in competition for the proposed canal terminus. Wolcott could not help but share the excitement over the economic benefits the canal would bring. In addition, the settlements at Maumee and Perrysburg at the Foot of the Rapids were already showing promise as centers of shipping and ship building. Willshire, on the other hand, was experiencing little commercial growth.

Wolcott apparently began to reconsider his financial options at this point. He could remain in Willshire and hope for improvement or he could take a chance on the down river communities on the Maumee River which were better located for commercial expansion. He chose the latter course and the Wolcotts left Willshire in 1826 and headed for the Maumee by way of Fort Wayne.

Meanwhile, James also became embroiled in a Wells family crisis which resulted in tragedy. In 1820, the price of government land had been reduced to $1.25 an acre and the government opened a land office in Fort Wayne three years later. The heirs of William Wells had never taken up their father's preemption rights at Wellsington. In 1826, reputedly on the advice of Wolcott, they agreed to divide the three hundred and twenty acres between the forks of the St. Mary and St. Joseph Rivers, known as the Wells Reserve. Anne had continued to live on the old homestead after her marriage and Rebecca and James Hackley resided on their small adjoining farm. Each agreed that should either of their sections be awarded to the other, they would mutually quit claim in order to maintain the status quo. When the division took place in the spring of 1826, Anne had a sudden change of mind. When she was awarded her sister's section, instead of abiding by the agreement, she attempted to take physical possession of the Hackley home. Hackley had no intention of surrendering his section . In a fit of rage he locked his wife in another room, attacked his sister-in-law, and according to some accounts, threatened to kill her. Anne is said to have escaped by leaping from an upstairs window. Later the same evening, the despondent Hackley, remorseful over what he had almost done, took his own life by hanging from a rafter in his home. He was discovered by two of his Masonic brothers, who also released his distraught wife. In spite of the circumstances surrounding his death, Hackley was given a respectable Masonic funeral service and was buried next to his daughter in the family burying ground at Wellsington. [31]

This sad turn of events took place toward the end of May, 1826, at about the time the Wolcotts were making preparation to leave for the Foot of the Rapids. It was a difficult time for a leave taking. Anne and Rebecca were both alone now and not surprisingly estranged from each other. Joseph McCoy, a Baptist minister and family friend, counseled Rebecca to "try to think the most favorable" as he had noted that her "peace seemed to be marred" with her sister and to "remember that she is bound in the bonds of affliction with you. . ."[32] William Wayne Wells was away, serving as a lieutenant in the Army and unable to provide any support to his sisters. Thus, James Wolcott, in addition to managing his wife's financial affairs, now took on the added responsibility of overseeing the estate of her sisters and absentee brother. He later explained that after marrying his wife, he found the estate of Wells to "consist of widows, minors and . . .children" and that "the task of defending their interest. . . very naturally fell to my lot." [33] Wolcott acquired power of attorney for Well's children by Sweet Breeze and acting on their behalf, apparently sold the remaining sections of land for a considerable profit. The division and sale of this land plus the escalating contention between the Wells children and their stepmother, Mary Wells Turner and her husband would lead to continuing litigation. The following year, Mary and Robert Turner filed suit in Jefferson County, Kentucky. In addition to the Wells children by Sweet Breeze, the suit named Samuel, Yelverton and Juliana, the children of William Wells and Mary Geiger Wells Turner as plaintiffs.

Little mention of Jane Wells is made during this period and no provision was made for her in Well's estate. However, as a half-blooded member of the Miami tribe, she received a half section of land along the Mississinewa River from the government in an 1826 treaty. Anne Turner and Rebecca Hackley also received a half-section each and Rebecca's children, Ann and Jack Hackley each received a full section. Mary Wells Wolcott was not named in the treaty which was signed on October 23, 1826. By that time, Mary and James, after a strenuous trip down river with their two young children and whatever household goods they could carry in an open boat, had already reached the settlement at Maumee. Wolcott presumably made prior arrangements with William Oliver to manage the Central House. The family temporarily resided at the hotel while Wolcott surveyed his prospects. Many former acquaintances and Wells family friends from Fort Wayne, including John Hunt and Robert Forsyth preceded them and all were heavily involved in trading and land speculation.

Mary Wells had been granted one section of land along the Wabash River in 1818 but as Indiana lands rose in value, the federal government rescinded the title and offered her eighteen hundred dollars in lieu of her original grant. Mary did not file her claim until after her marriage and in 1827, Wolcott invested this money in the purchase of River Tracts 20, 21, 28 and 30 in Waynesfield Township from the United States government. Although this land was purchased in the name of James rather than Mary, Wolcott later explained that it was with the "express understanding and agreement" between husband and wife and that it was purchased for her benefit. [34] Lots 21 and 20 contained three hundred acres of prime real estate between the Maumee River and the projected canal route. The property also fronted on the "Great Trail," the oldest and most heavily traveled route between Detroit and Fort Wayne. Wolcott immediately began construction of a story and a half log house on lot 21 overlooking the Maumee River. Docks and warehouses were appearing all along the river banks and Wolcott lost no time in constructing his own commercial buildings at the foot of lot 21. He divided his other tracts into town lots and would record "Wolcott's Addition" to "Miami City" in 1837.

The promise of the canal attracted many investors, land speculators and others of enterprising mind to the Foot of the Rapids. These early entrepreneurs recognized that the success of their commercial investments depended in large part on developing a stable community and providing amenities to attract new residents and investors.

Wolcott quickly joined the ranks of his civic minded neighbors and accepted appointment as a "road viewer" in 1837. This position was consistent with his views on internal improvements and government support for establishing efficient systems of transportation throughout the West. This was one of many issues on which he differed with President Andrew Jackson and Jackson's successor, Martin Van Buren. Jackson's fiscal policies, including the elimination of the local and state banks and his Specie Circular which curtailed the speculative activity in the Maumee Valley as elsewhere throughout the West were particularly irksome for Wolcott and his fellow entrepreneurs. Wolcott's own financial success had been slow but steady. By 1836, his legal agent, Nathan Rathbun, wrote that he had been carrying his client through the hard times but he now felt that Wolcott's business interests were stable enough that he could finally charge him for what he was "rightly due." He did admit that during this lean period, Wolcott had occasionally supplied him with fresh hams and produce, a common medium of exchange on the frontier.[35] Indeed, by the following year, Wolcott was said to be "doing a business in the grocery line almost exclusively wholesale," and the editor of the local newssheet promised that "his sales will not suffer in comparison with any other establishment along the river." The Forwarding and Commissioning business was flourishing in Maumee and advertisements for "James Wolcott and Co., Forwarding and Commissioning Merchants" were found regularly in the Maumee Express. Many of Wolcott's commercial rivals, including Hunt and Forsyth, served as agents for larger shipping companies. In 1838, Wolcott announced that in partnership with A.J. Hackley of New York and James Howe, he was acting agent for the shipping lines of National Line, New York, Buffalo, Utica and Buffalo and Oswego Lines. Between 1833 and 1843, ship carpenters turned out a record number of schooners and steamboats for local entrepreneurs, including two for Wolcott.

Wolcott was in the vanguard of those who applied for a municipal charter for the village of Maumee. The first election was held in March, 1838. Residents chose Robert Forsyth as their first mayor. Wolcott was elected to represent the third ward or "Miami" in the village council. As an indication of the respect in which he was held by his contemporaries, Wolcott was elected the first president of the Maumee council. The same year, he was also elected associate judge of the Lucas County court. Due to the great difficulty in traveling between settlements, the Ohio constitution provided for three supreme court justices appointed by the legislature to hold court annually in each county. In between visits, three associate judges could hear cases when presided over by a circuit judge. Although Lucas County had been established in1836, there was as yet no courthouse and court was held in various buildings in Toledo. Wolcott was one of a group of Maumee entrepreneurs who dedicated their efforts toward construction of a courthouse and county buildings in Maumee. By the time Lucas County voters elected to establish the county seat in Maumee in 1840, construction of the stately Greek Revival courthouse was completed and open for public business.

Wolcott's political interests ranged beyond local issues and his strong opposition to Jackson's policies led him to become one of the founders of the Lucas County Whig Party. In 1838, the local Whigs were garnering support for Wolcott's old friend, Henry Clay, against the incumbent president, Martin Van Buren. Wolcott, in his capacity as chairman of the Whig party, authored a lengthy treatise in the <u>Maumee Express</u> in which he accused the present Democratic administration of corruption on many levels, particularly in the destruction of the banking system. He extolled the virtues of Henry Clay and appealed to Ohioans to support the Whig platform. That same year, Wolcott traveled as Lucas County delegate to the state convention to place Clay's name in nomination. The delegates, however, chose another westerner, William Well's old comrade, William Henry Harrison, to carry their standard. Although disappointed for Clay, Wolcott continued his support of the Whigs and their chosen candidate.

As the campaign heated up, Wolcott launched his first steamboat in May, 1840 from his Miami dock. The 350 ton ship was appropriately christened the "General Harrison" and the occasion was celebrated with cannon salute and many hurrahs from the crowd which was composed of "almost the entire population of this and the neighboring towns.". Wolcott did not overlook the political significance of the event and the ship's deck was festooned with groves of buckeye trees in full bloom, a broken slippery elm symbolizing Van Buren's down fall, and a sheaf of wheat with various agricultural implements to represent the "country yeoman." Perhaps the most important element to many of the onlookers was the large barrel of hard cider lashed upon the "windlass bitts" which the revelers were invited to sample freely. The Express gave hearty approval to Wolcott's efforts and applauded his "enterprize(sic) and energy." [36] The voters of Maumee expressed their approval of Wolcott when they elected him mayor of Maumee on March 27, 1843.

Commercial activity was at its height at the Foot of the Rapids between 1835 and 1850. Observers predicted that Maumee would become the leading lake port on the western Great Lakes. Over sixteen mercantile establishments in the village of Maumee and a similar number in Perrysburg were stocked with merchandise and competed for the local and transient trade. The General Harrison, commanded by Captain I.T. Pheatt was one of many ships carrying goods and passengers between the Foot of the Rapids, Detroit, Sandusky and Buffalo on a daily basis and it would be joined by Wolcott's second ship, the James Wolcott in 1843.

Wolcott's fortunes continued to improve as the community grew and prospered. The shipping and forwarding business was at its peak and as the population expanded, his general merchandise store was kept busy supplying customers. A little business community grew up around the Upper Steamboat Landing where Wolcott's wharves, warehouse and ships were located. He could gaze out of the front room of his home and watch the bustling activity on the river front while from the other direction, he could hear the husky voices of the packet boat pilots along the canal, barking orders to their crews. A sidecut linked the canal with the river, running through the eastern edge of Wolcott's property and at the bottom of the hill, Wolcott and John Hunt built a mill operated by water power. In addition, his real estate interests were proving profitable and the sale of lots in Wolcott's addition was on the increase.. The prosperity he had worked for was finally materializing but at the height of Wolcott's financial success, the family lost wife and mother, Mary Wells Wolcott, an important link in her father and grandfather's vision of uniting the two cultures.

While James Wolcott found success in the world of politics and commerce, Mary Wells Wolcott was the keeper of the home fires. Mary had spent her adolescent years in the comfort of her Uncle Samuel's spacious Greek Revival home, surrounded by family and numerous friends. Slavery was a part of plantation life and her every need was attended to. Parties, balls and visiting occupied the leisure time of the southern belle and was the life Mary had been prepared for. Instead, she had chosen to follow her husband to struggling frontier communities where the amenities were few and life was full of challenges. From the pioneer settlement at Willshire to the more promising river port of Maumee City, she shared equally in the hardships of frontier living. Her world revolved around husband, home and family. She bore seven children in a relatively short time. Following William Wells and Robert Fulton, Mary Ann, the Wolcott's third child and only surviving daughter was born in 1827. Three years later, Henry Clay was born, followed by Frederic Allyn in 1843 and James Monroe in 1839. Robert Fulton died at the young age of twelve and the Wolcott's also lost a three week old infant. Mary's religious faith sustained her through these tragedies. Her son, James Monroe, later noted that his "mother was a devout Christian and a zealous Episcopalian." [37] Although she grew up among the southern Baptists in Kentucky, the Wells family had been Episcopalians and Mary continued that tradition. There was no Episcopal Church in northwest Ohio when the Wolcotts arrived and Mary prevailed upon James to build a small log chapel on their property. Son James later stated that "Ma built herself the first church..." The Reverend Burton Hicox held "divine services" every Sunday afternoon in the chapel after preaching to a small congregation in Toledo (later Trinity) and neighboring Episcopalians were welcome to attend services. In 1837, Wolcott and several others donated a lot at the corner of East Wayne and Elizabeth Streets for construction of a church. St. Pauls Episcopal Church was completed in 1841 and four generations of Wolcotts would attend religious services and participate in church related activities. Mary practiced her religious precepts .Her obituary notes that "the poor and destitute" are deprived of "a kind and beneficent friend, who was ever ready to sympathize in their afflictions and relieve their wants." The writer notes that although "she often dried up the tears of other fellow beings, the only ones that she caused to flow were those at her departure."

Mary appears to have slowly drifted apart from her siblings. Although packet boats regularly carried passengers and mail back and forth from Fort Wayne, there is no evidence of correspondence or physical contact between the sisters. Anne and Rebecca resolved their estrangement and quietly lived out their lives in Fort Wayne where they were seen together regularly at Presbyterian church services and were said to hold a "fine social position among our best people."[38] Mary and her sisters attempted to remain in touch with their brother, Wayne, who had a promising career in the military. He had graduated fourth in his class from West Point and was commissioned a first Lieutenant in 1825. A letter to his sister, Rebecca in 1828, however, indicates that Wayne was becoming disillusioned with military life. He apologized for his neglect in writing to his "dear sister," pointing to "causes and anxieties" too depressing to explain. Although he would like to offer assistance to Rebecca in her bereavement, he confessed that his "wayward disposition" places such "happiness beyond my reach for the present." Wayne wrote from Fort Monroe on the eastern coast of Virginia while awaiting assignment to a yet undisclosed post. In poor health and a heavy drinker, a common malady among military officers stationed in isolated areas, he resigned his commission in 1831. He died of cholera the following year while on the steamer <u>Superior</u> near Erie, Pennsylvania. The administration of his estate was granted to James Wolcott. His "sheepskin"(diploma), ceremonial sword and land which he earlier wrote that he had not yet disposed of, were left to Mary. Two years later, Anne Turner died. In 1827, Jacob Geiger had written to Ann, suggesting that she seek assistance in her legal affairs from James Wolcott. and her government allotment also descended to her youngest sister. That same year, Rebecca received a quarter section of land in the Treaty of the Forks of the Wabash. [39] Rebecca died in June of 1835, shortly after her daughter, Ann, was married to Nathan Ferrand, leaving Mary as the only surviving child of Sweet Breeze and William Wells.

Mary left no records of her excursions beyond the circle of family and church and no letters or diaries to provide a glimpse into her private life. When she died in February, 1843, her obituary accurately noted that her "husband has been deprived of an affectionate wife. Her children of an indulgent but judicious mother." At age 43, she had outlived two children and all of her siblings. It was not until July that her nephew, Jack Hackley, then a student at Indiana University, conveyed the news of the "melancholy death of Aunt Wolcott" to her half sister, Jane Wells Griggs.

Mary Wells Wolcott was interred in the family burial plot directly below her home on a bluff overlooking the Maumee River, in February, 1843. Even her final resting place is shrouded in mystery. When eroding riverbanks made it necessary to move the family grave sites to Riverside Cemetery, Mary's headstone could not be found. Her only existing monument to posterity is in the stately home which she and James built.

James Wolcott.
Portrait by Walter Chapman from the original minature in possession of the Lucas County/Maumee Valley Historical Society.

An unusual hollow cut silhouette on black silk, believed to be Mary Wells Wolcott.
LC/MVHS

Wolcott Genealogy

James Wolcott (Mary Wells)
b. 11/3/1789 Torrington, Connecticut
d 1/5/1873 Maumee, Ohio
|
Guy Wolcott (Abigail Allyn)
b 8/7/1760 Windsor, Conn.
d 10/5/1781 Tallmadge, Ohio
|
Alexander Wolcott, M.D. (Mary Richards)
b 5/7/1712
d 3/25/1795 Windsor, Conn.
|
Roger Wolcott (Sarah Drake)
b 1/4/1679
d 5/17/1757 Windsor, Conn.
|
Simon Wolcott (Martha Pitkin)
b 1625 England
d 1687 Windsor, Conn.
|
Henry Wolcott (Elizabeth Saunders)
b 1578 England
d 5/30/1655 Windsor, Conn.
|
John Wolcott
Tolland, Somerset, England

Marriage License of James and Mary Wolcott

I hereby certify that the Marriage covenant was duely solemnized by me according to the Laws of the State of Missouri between Mr. James Wolcott and Miss Mary Wells of said State County of St. Charles and Township of Lower Cuiver, on this 8th day of March – In the year of our Lord 1821 — Charles S. Robinson an ordained Clergyman

Witnesses Present
Sam. Wells
James [illegible]
Nathan Heald

Mary Ann Wolcott Gilbert, daughter of James and Mary Wolcott.
LC/MVHS

Smith Gilbert. Husband of Mary Ann   LC/MVHS

Mary Ann Wolcott Gilbert and daughter Fredericka dressed in "Indian" costume. James M. later related that they often dressed in makeshift costumes.

Fredericka Gilbert Hull
LC/MVHS

William Hull, husband of Fredericka. LC/MVHS

Rilla Hull, daughter of Fredericka and William Hull

Zoe and Ella Wolcott, daughters of William Wolcott

Wolcott House. C. 1890's.

Portion of map of Maumee, Ohio, 1875 showing "James Wolcott Estate" and Wolcott Street.

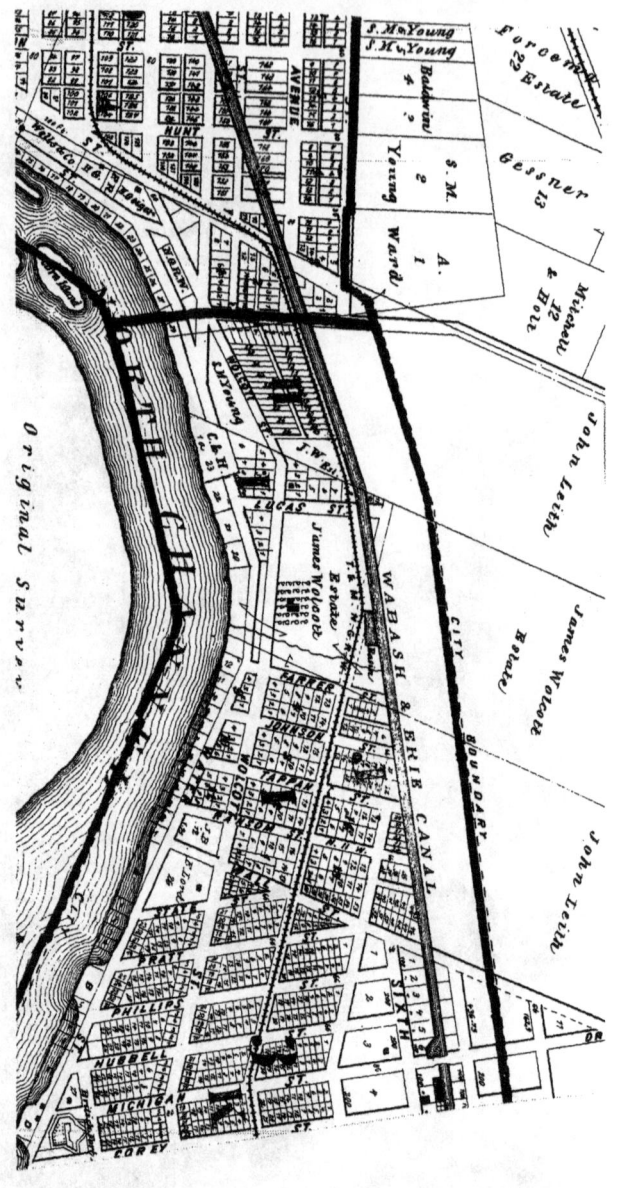

Lithograph of Wolcott's steamer, General Harrison.
LC/MVHS

Ledger page from **General Harrison** Account Book William Wolcott is given as master.

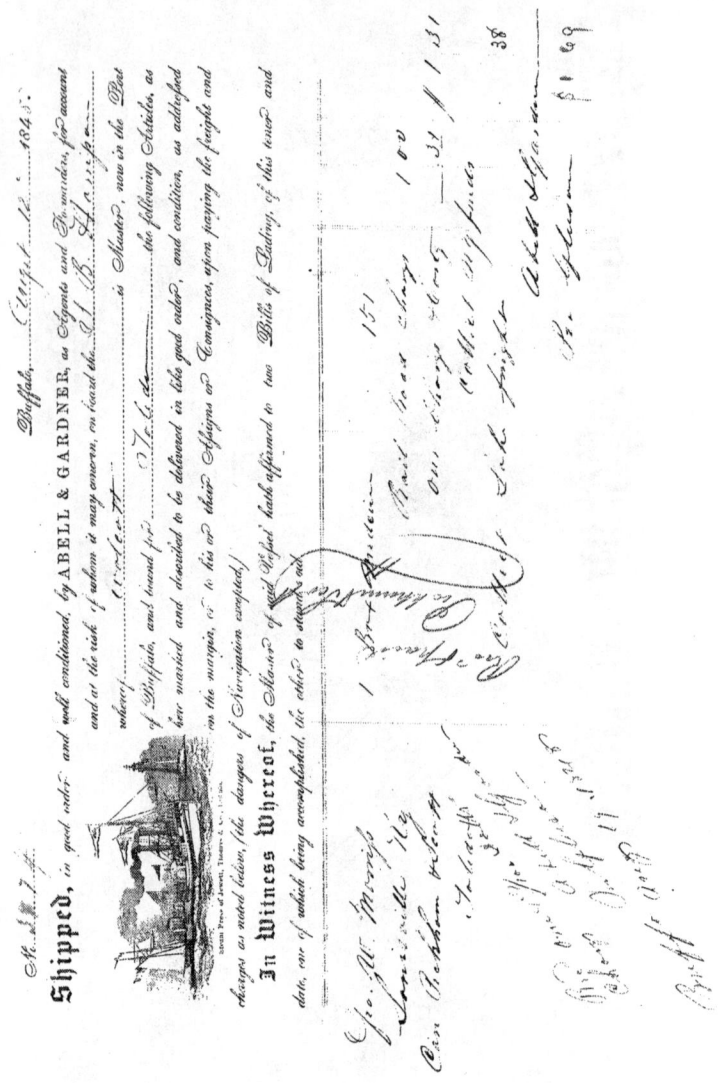

St. Paul's Episcopal Church built in 1843. James was among the founders and four generations worshiped here.

Lucas County Courthouse built in 1840. James Wolcott was among the contributors toward its construction in 1840.

IV

Epilogue

The Next Generations

After a respectable mourning period, James wed Caroline B. Davis on November 21, 1844. The new bride, widow of a Toledo attorney, found herself in charge of a busy household and mother to five step children. They ranged in age from four year old James Monroe to twenty-two year old William. As the oldest son, William intended to go to college but after the death of his mother he determined to follow a career on the lakes and ultimately became the captain of the General Harrison Mary Ann, who had resumed her mother's domestic duties and helped care for her younger siblings in the interim before her father's re-marriage, was quickly dispatched to the. Ontario Female Seminary in Canandaigua, New York to study music and art. In 1845, Caroline gave birth to James's eighth child, Joseph Lake Wolcott. The fourteen rooms of the Wolcott House were filled to capacity with parents, children and two live-in servants. Apparently life was not idyllic, however, and James Wolcott's second marriage lasted little more than a decade. Divorce was considered a drastic and often scandalous action in the nineteenth century. To take such a step indicated irreconcilable differences in the relationship.

If those differences were the result of friction between stepdaughter and stepmother, that problem was removed when Mary Ann married Smith Gilbert in 1848 and left the family homestead. William had married Eliza Border in February of that year and the young couple began their married life as boarders with Mrs. Pheatt, a family friend. Eventually, with daughters, Zoe, Effie and son Bryan, they moved into their own nearby home. With the departure of Caroline and little Joseph, Mary Ann once again assumed the responsibilities as mistress of her father' household which now included her own children, Fredericka (1850), Albert (1852) and Smith, Jr. (1854), and husband Smith, Sr., in addition to her younger brothers, Frederick, Henry Clay and James.

Mary Ann cared for her father until his death in 1873. James Wolcott lived to see his fortune ebb away during his lifetime, probably as a result of over speculation during the height of the canal boom and it appears he had little to leave to his children other than the family homestead and his original land purchase which had been valued for its close proximity to the canal and the river front. However, by the mid-1850's, the promise of the canal was beginning to prove false as railroads were found to be cheaper, faster and not subject to geographical restrictions. Morever, Maumee was losing its distinction as the leading center of shipping as newer, larger vessels found the channel too shallow to navigate up-river. Although account books of the steamer, <u>General Harrison</u>, show a lively trade between Buffalo and Maumee, Wolcott sold a half interest in the ship to an investor when the forwarding business began to decline. For several years, boosters of Maumee and Toledo had engaged in an intense commercial and political rivalry. Maumee had the earlier advantage but by 1846, Toledo succeeded in removing the customs house to their city and in 1852, Maumee also lost the coveted county seat designation. Many of Wolcott's contemporaries, such as John Hunt, Jessup Scott and William Oliver, followed their economic instincts and abandoned Maumee for the faster growing city while the Wolcotts continued to keep faith with Maumee's future. James had divided his additional tracts of land into approximately 150 town lots but the lake trade was moving down river by 1860 and the promising city of Maumee was becoming a "sleepy village." James turned his efforts to improving his farmlands and is listed in the 1850 census as "farmer" rather than merchant. Ten years earlier, the census had recorded two Wolcott family members engaged in commerce and one in navigation but none in agriculture. Hired hands had performed the necessary farm chores at that time, but Frederick and Henry, willingly or not, would soon find themselves learning the art of husbandry.

Farming was left behind, however, as civil war erupted between North and South. Frederick and Henry, who had likely been training with the Waynesfield Guards marched off to defend the Union. James M.(Tip) joined the 130th Regiment when it was organized in 1864 and quickly advanced to sergeant, first class. Even their young half brother, Joseph, too young to enlist, was caught up in the patriotic furor and signed on as a drummer boy. James, Sr. and William, who were over age for the draft, were among the Lucas County residents who signed a declaration in support of the Union soldiers when military morale fell exceptionally low in 1863. Mary Ann's husband, Smith Gilbert, did not see military service but as a three term mayor of Maumee, steered the community through the difficult war years. While her brothers were at the front, Mary Ann was busy as a founding member of the Women's Relief Society which met weekly and sometimes daily to roll bandages and pack kits for soldiers. She kept her brother's spirits high by writing letters and occasionally sending them a "novelette." They, in turn, sent their pay home in care of their brother-in-law, Mayor Gilbert. All but William would see action and all but Frederick, who was killed near Atlanta in July, 1864 during Sherman's "march to the sea", would return to their father' home. Joseph served throughout the duration of the war after coming of age and returned to become a prominent Toledo businessman.

James Wolcott continued with the legal counsel of his attorney, Nathan Rathbun, to attempt a satisfactory settlement of his late wife's affairs. Even before Mary's death, James had to sell some of Ann Turner's lands to pay off outstanding debts against her estate. Squatters on the Indiana lands presented another problem and court action sometimes had to be taken to protect family claims. Even after the death of James in 1873, Mary Ann and James M. wrote to E.D. Peck, congressman from Toledo, thanking him for past kindnesses and requesting assistance in surveying and removing squatters from their Uncle Wayne's lands. Moreover, the heirs of the children of William Wells by his second wife took up the Turner's law suits against the children of Sweet Breeze. The situation was complicated when Mary Geiger Wells Turner divorced her husband Robert Turner, who claimed to be guardian of Wells estate, and settlement was further delayed with the deaths of Turner, Samuel Wells and his agent, Peyton Wells, and William Wells's daughter from his second marriage, Juliana Wells. The estate remained in litigation for over twenty years.

In 1847, Mary's niece, Ann Hackley Ferrand, who had been widowed the previous year, and her brother Jack had given Wolcott power of attorney to manage their affairs. Shortly thereafter, Ann married Peter Blystone and the couple moved to Lucas County where Peter also had relatives. Peter served on the Monclova Board of Education and Ann joined the Presbyterian Church. For the first time in many years, descendants of William Wells became neighbors. First cousins Mary Ann and Ann apparently shared a warm, if brief, friendship. In 1854, Jack Hackley was one of five delegates who negotiated the Treaty of Washington with the Miami which provided for an allotment of two hundred acres of land in Kansas for each head of an eligible household.[40] Jack died before he could receive his allotment but in the spring of 1857, Ann and Peter left friends and family and set out for the far west to choose their homesite. The following spring, after spending the winter on the Miami Mission (where Ann curiously noted that they would have remained longer "had it not been for the Indians"), Ann wrote a lengthy letter to her cousin describing the virtues of their new farm.[41] Their good fortune no doubt evoked a bit of envy among Mary Ann and her brothers as well as resentment that they had not been included in the treaty provisions. They renewed their efforts to press the government for what they felt was their fair share due them through their mother and Uncle Wayne. In 1870, they petitioned to have their names entered on the Miami Indian rolls, pointing out that their Indiana cousins had received generous settlements. Unfortunately, they could be included only by tribal consent and the tribal council had ceased to assemble. William appears to have been particularly bitter and as late as 1882 complained that "we are the only descendants of the Miamis who have received from the Government nothing." This, he added, was because their father "paid no attention to our interests in these lands, appropriations and annuities" [42] Finally, in 1888, the Department of Indian Affairs notified the Wolcott heirs through their agent, H.G. Norton, that all lands and annuities due to Mary Wells Wolcott had been distributed before her death and nothing more was due them.

James Wolcott passed away in his home "of no perceptible cause" but "simply worn out with old age," on January 5, 1873. At his passing, he was still considered among the esteemed citizens and pioneers of the Maumee Valley. The <u>Toledo Commercial</u> devoted almost an entire column to his life and accomplishments. The <u>Commercial</u> noted that he was respected as a "good citizen" and a man of "good character and habits." Although he "was not at that time an (active) member of any church," possibly as a result of his earlier divorce, his service was delivered by the Reverend T.N. Barkdull, as was duly noted by the local newspapers.[43] At eighty four years of age, Wolcott had outlived many of his competitors and contemporaries and had left an enduring monument for future generations.

The descendants of James and Mary would continue to be

stewards of their family homestead for the next three generations, not always without contention. William, even before his father's death, contested the right of Mary Ann and her husband to inhabit the homestead. The question was settled through several court actions. Ultimately, the Court determined that the land, in intent, was purchased for the benefit of Mary Wells Wolcott and her descendants and should be divided equally among them. Mary Ann and James M. shared ownership of tract 21 which included the family home. The tract was partitioned in 1875 and Mary Ann received the section "east of the Garden Fence" lying between the canal (Anthony Wayne Trail) and Wolcott Street containing the family home and all outbuildings. In return, Mary Ann paid her brother $612.50 as compensation for his receiving the smaller allotment. Although the issue of ownership of the family homestead was settled in court, personal differences took longer to heal and William appears to have remained estranged from James M. and Mary Ann

The sons of James Wolcott followed in their father's footsteps in many respects. William inherited James's mechanical bent of mind. During the "gas boom" of the 1880's, William invented and submitted a patent for a self regulating gas valve for oil drilling rigs. Unfortunately the gas boom was over by the turn of the century. William's only venture into politics was an unsuccessful bid for councilman of the third ward when his son Byron ran for Assessor, both on the Democratic ticket. Ironically, this election took place in 1887, the same year that his brother James was elected mayor on the Republican ticket. William navigated the lakes for several years as captain of some of the finest steamboats. In his later years, he served as a night watchman and lamplighter in the third ward of Maumee and augmented his income by selling off some of his land. At his death in 1904 at the age of 84, his obituary noted that "he was a man of fine conversational powers, his wonderful memory enabling him to relate many an incident of the early pioneer days." Like his mother, he was said to be "kind and generous...a good friend and neighbor." [44]

James M., nicknamed "Tip" for William Henry Harrison's campaign slogan "Tippecanoe and Tyler, Too," was a popular member of the community and followed his father into politics. He was elected mayor of Maumee in 1887 and 1897, was Justice of the Peace for many years and served a term as Lucas County Clerk Tip was a member of the Grand Army of the Republic, the Northern Light Masonic Lodge and the Maumee Valley Pioneer Association. There is no record of any marriage and he was still living on the homestead with his widowed sister, his occupation given as "Dentist" in the 1880 census. Tip, like his brother, William, was proud of his Miami heritage and enjoyed sharing family legends with various groups, including the Eighth Annual Reunion of the Society of Descendants of Henry Wolcott which he addressed in Detroit in 1912 when he was seventy-three years old. He kept up a correspondence with the Secretary of the Chicago Historical Society and generously donated several family relics to that organization. Tip continued to live in the family home and took great pride in his orchards, prompting a local columnist to note that while serving as mayor, he generously shared his first peaches of the season with his many friends. . At his death in 1917, at the age of seventy-eight, he had outlived all his siblings.

Little is known of Henry Clay. In 1869 he gave up all his claims to the family property in favor of his brother, William. He died in 1882, still unmarried at the age of 51.

Mary Ann, described as "graceful" with "very dark hair, a piercing eye," and a "firm, quick step" continued to oversee the Wolcott homestead after her husband's death in 1879. [45] In addition to her brother Tip, her daughter, Fredericka, (presumably named for her brother, Frederick), Fredericka's husband, William Hull and their daughter, Rilla born in 1880, also made their home with her. After Mary Ann's death in 1891, the home descended to Fredericka, or "Freddie" as she was familiarly called. Freddie appears to have inherited some of the willfulness and determination of her great grandfather, William Wells. It was said that when a doctor advised her to discontinue drinking coffee and eating meat, she defied him by increasing her consumption of coffee and eating meat three times a day. When she died in 1934 at the age of eighty-four, it was reported that although she had been in ill health for several years she had refused to "keep to her bed." Fredericka was a dedicated worker for the Episcopal Church and a pillar of the Women's Relief Corp. Although she was given a traditional funeral service, an American Legion military honor guard accompanied her to her final resting place in the family burial plot.

Rilla, or "Rill," the only child of Fredericka and William Hull, lived her entire life in the ancestral home. After her mother's death, Rilla continued to maintain what remained of the family estate and to keep alive memories of "past greatness." She was proud of her heritage and passed on many anecdotes, often enhanced by generations of story tellers. Like her mother and grandmothers, Rilla was a tireless worker in St. Paul's Episcopal Church and enjoyed working in the kitchen for parish dinners and other activities. She was devoted to a succession of dogs, and parishioners recall that her faithful pet always accompanied her to church, curled up beside her on the pew throughout the service. The Wolcott fortune was a faint memory during Rilla's lifetime with only the Wolcott House as a tangible reminder of the family's once powerful presence in the valley. However, Rilla was determined to preserve the house and its artifacts as a tribute to the pioneer past. Since it was not acceptable for women to work outside the home, Rilla solved the problem by becoming a long distance operator for the local telephone company, operating from a switchboard in her own house. In later years, as it became more difficult to maintain her home, she took in boarders. They are recalled as a rather unlikely pair - one a ticket taker at a Toledo Burlesque House and other an employee of the nearby race track. It was said that she never introduced them to her friends and never made explanations for them. Over the years, Rilla was forced to make some difficult concessions. Upstairs room arrangements were altered to accommodate the boarders and it was sometimes necessary to sell family pieces such as the original brasses from the dining room sideboard. When Rilla died in 1957, she had only eighty nine dollars in her checking account but she had achieved her goal of saving the Wolcott House for future generations. Rilla had often shared her dream of a museum with neighbors and friends and she willed title to the property to St. Paul's Episcopal Church with the request that her goal be fulfilled. The Church retained the river front property but transferred the house and remaining property to the City of Maumee who agreed to lease the property to the Maumee Valley Historical Society. After extensive fund raising efforts led by the Historical Society and wide spread support from the community, the Wolcott House Museum officially opened to the public in 1960.

Family of James and Mary Wolcott

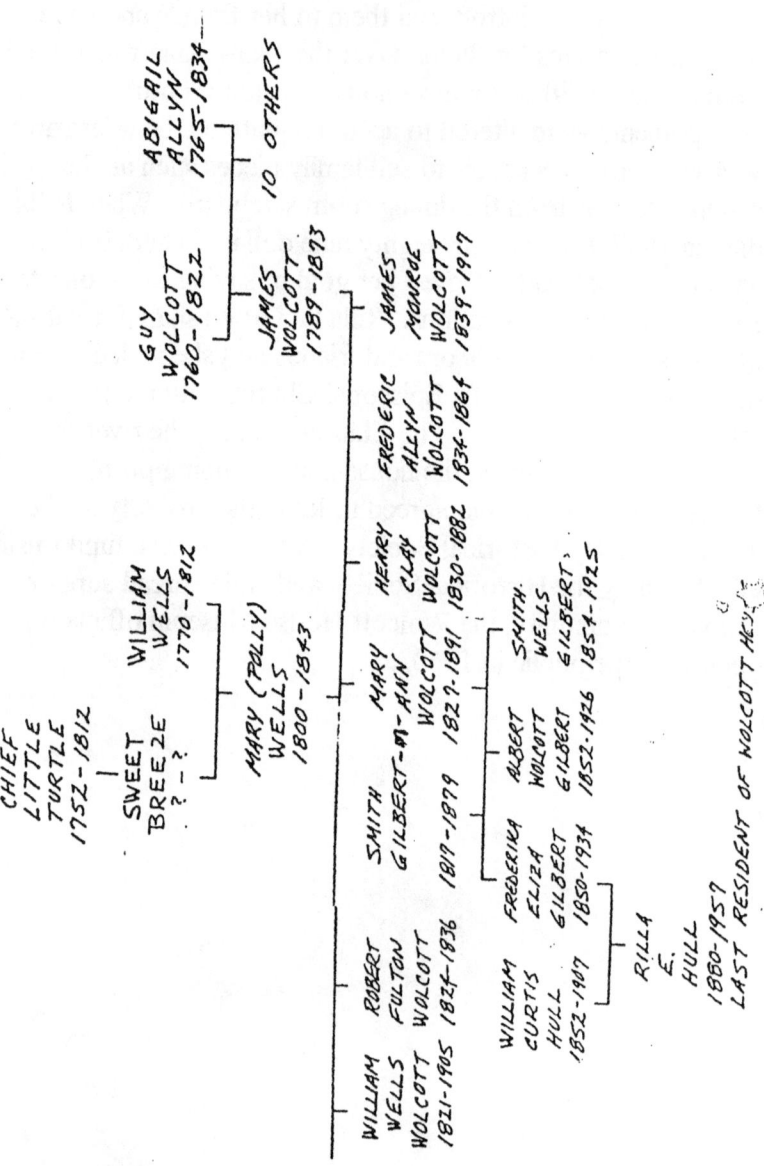

Members of the Grand Army of the Republic, c. 1900s.
"Tip" Wolcott, fifth from left, top row.
Author's collection.

Women's Relief Corp, c. 1888. Mary Ann Wolcott Gilbert, top row, far left. Fredericka Gilbert Hull, standing, bottom row, extreme left.
Author's collection.

The rift between brothers extended into their political activities. In 1887, James was successful in his bid for Mayor on the Republican ticket. William and his son, Byron, also ran for municipal office, unsuccessfully, under the Democratic Party's standard as seen in this 1887 ballot.

DEMOCRAT TICKET.

3d Ward.

For Treasurer,
J. A. CHURCH.

For Marshal,
PHILLIP HARTMAN.

For Street Commissioner,
PETER BICK.

For Cemetery Trustee,
WM. RECTENWALL.

For Councilman,
W. W. WOLCOTT.

For Assessor,
BYRON WOLCOTT.

For Gas Trustees,
J. W. PAUKEN,

P. CHRISTIE.

Township.

For Trustee,
P. CHRISTIE.

For Clerk,
U. B. TALYOR.

For Supervisor,
MOTTS BRIER.

Rilla Hull enjoyed sharing stories and artifacts from her family's collection.

Wayne Baldwin, a descendant of Mary Wells Wolcott, William Wells and Chief Little Turtle kept the family tradition alive during the 1960's by performing Native American dances and sharing the Miami culture.

Chapter V

THE LEGACY

The simple log cabin that James and Mary built on the banks of the Maumee River over one hundred and seventy years ago gradually evolved to meet the needs of an expanding family and reflected Wolcott's growing prosperity and importance in the community. Included in the original two story addition are a dining room and a parlor, each with formal fireplaces leading to chimneys on opposite gabled ends. A particularly interesting feature is the recessed alcove next to the parlor fireplace, rarely seen in northwest Ohio but common in southern homes and designed to accommodate large pieces of furniture. A graceful front entranceway is flanked by sidelights with bent wooden trim resembling wrought iron, a technique found in the pattern books of eastern architect, Asher Benjamin. The doorway opens into a central hall where a door at the opposite end once provided cross ventilation on hot summer days. A frosted glass oil lamp still hangs by the winding black walnut free standing staircase to the second floor where another door centered over the main entrance opens to cool river breezes. Over the years, a formal dining room was added behind the parlor and the original dining/sitting room became a study for Wolcott where he could conduct business and entertain associates, including an increasing number of political cronies, as he became more involved in community life. The study is paneled in the same black walnut used throughout the house. A handsome cherry desk, possibly crafted by a nearby cabinetmaker, fits into the recess in the bookcase wall which is thought to have housed the original kitchen fireplace. Wolcott soon replaced inefficient fireplace heating with a more advanced "Franklin" heating stove. By the time of its completion, the original log cabin was barely discernible within the spacious home, a showplace for its day.

The surrounding grounds also underwent improvement as additional land was cleared. A summer kitchen was located nearby and a stable large enough to house Wolcott's two horses, a buggy and a sleigh was constructed a convenient distance from the main house. Wolcott, like most of his neighbors, managed a self sufficient farm which provided his family with all the essentials for daily life. Numerous outbuildings, including barns, storage sheds, smoke house and chicken coops were still in use on the premises into the twentieth century. Chicken, hogs and fourteen head of cattle wandered the barnyard. Because livestock often strayed onto neighboring property, owners branded or cropped their ears and entered their "earmark" in the public record. Wolcott established his ownership with a distinctive "J.W."

Fields of corn, wheat and flax spread across the rear of the property and the Wolcott's maintained a large orchard composed of peach as well as apple trees.

As Wolcott enlarged the main house, he excavated an underground "cellar" with outside doorways large enough to allow access for a wagon and other large farm equipment. The cellar had a dirt floor and a fireplace ample enough to accommodate the many daily and seasonal household activities. Although meals could be prepared in a summer kitchen or upstairs, possibly on a "Perfect Premium" iron cookstove widely used in the 1830's and likely available in Wolcott's stores, many of the activities related to fall butchering and harvesting could be carried out in the spacious cellar. The weekly laundry also could be boiled and dried near the fire in inclement weather. During the hot summer months, the cellar provided a cool workroom for Mary and her helpers to make candles and soap for the family's use. In later years, because of Mary's family affiliation with the Miami, it was rumored that the cellar was left open for wandering Indians. However, by the time the cellar room was added, most of the Native Americans had left or were leaving northwest Ohio and they were primarily of Ottawa and not Miami descent. As noted earlier, although Mary was proud of her heritage, she had little contact with her Indian relatives during her youth and even less with the Miami who lived around Fort Wayne. Still, given the nature of her generous disposition, travelers may have been welcome in the Wolcott home.

The finishing touch to the "Mansion" was the addition of the two story porticoed veranda, smaller in size but reminiscent of her Uncle Samuel's Kentucky home. The graceful supporting columns were turned by R.J. McMurray, a local cabinetmaker whose shop was located a short distance up river.

As Mary Well's life represents a blending of cultures, her home stands as a blending of architectural styles and regional tastes, suggesting both the prevailing Federal simplicity of James Wolcott's New England roots and the classical lines of Mary's southern Kentucky heritage. Today, the Wolcott House remains relatively unchanged and is a tribute to both the Native American inhabitants and the early settlers of the lower Maumee Valley.

Home of Samuel Wells in Louisville where Mary spent her youth showing the remarkable similarity between the entryways of the Kentucky home and the Wolcott home in Maumee, particularly in the sidelights with bent wood insets.

The Wolcott House Museum, 2002.

END NOTES

1. Colonel Pope, in addition to his own family, brought his sister, Jane Pope Holmes and her husband and children. Colonel Oldham was single when he joined the travelers but married a daughter of Pope, who he had met on the journey, soon after arrival at the "falls." The Pope family would be among the members of the most prominent and powerful circles in Louisville which also included families of George Rogers Clark,, John Floyd, Frederick Geiger and Samuel Wells.

2. Carter, Harvey Lewis, The Life and Times of Little Turtle, First Sagamore of the Wabash, p 115.

3. Volney, Constantin F., A View of the Soil and Climate Of the United States of America, p. 406.

4. Ibid.

5. Ibid.

6. Carter, p. 115. This incident is discussed in several works.

7. Hutton, p. 193, Carter, p. 121.

8. Memoir of Charles Wells, Wolcott Collection.

9. Knopf, Richard C., <u>Campaign in the Wilderness,</u> Pp. 63,64.

10. Volney p. 426.

11. Wright, Richard, <u>John Hunt Memoirs,</u> p, 38.

12. Carter, p. 163.

13. Walker, Joseph E., "Plowshares and Pruning Hooks For the Miami," p.383.

14. Unidentified officer's observation in Cramton, Willa , <u>Women Beyond the Frontier,</u>

15. Carter, p. 203

16. Ibid.

17. Wright, pp. 34,35.

18. Manuscript Collection, Ohio Historical Society Archives

19. These items are on display at the Fort Wayne Historical Society Museum.

20. Volney, pp. 430,431.

21. Meuter, Maria Kitty, The Long Rifle, The Bow and The Calumet., p. 55.

22. Wright, p. 38.

23. Correspondence between the children of William Wells can be found in the Wells Family Collection a t Fort Wayne Historical Society

24. Carter, p. 249.

25. The following references attributed to members of the Wells family are found in the Wells Family File at the Fort Wayne Historical Society. See below.*

26. Wolcott Collection, Lucas County/Maumee Valley Historical Society.

27. Moyers-Johnson, Mary, "In Transition - The Family of Rebecca Wells Hackley."

28. Carter gives September 27, 1837 as Turner's death but Anne and her husband had apparently separated a decade earlier.

29. Alig, Joyce, Ohio's Last Frontiersman, pp 197-200. Alig documents the Wolcott's years at Willshire.

30. Ibid.

31. This incident is discussed in several Fort Wayne histories including Dawson, James, "Charcoal Sketches," p.2.

32. James McCoy to Rebecca Hackley, October 7, 1826.

33. James Wolcott to heirs of Juliana Wells.

34. Wolcott Collection, Court Records.

35. Journal of Nathan Rathbun, unpaginated

36. Maumee Express, May 16, 1840.

37. Historical Sketch by James M. Wolcott for the Society of Descendants of Henry Wolcott, 1912. Wolcott Collection.

38. Dawson, p 2

39. Moyers-Johnson

40. Ibid

41. Ann Hackley Blystone to Mary Ann Gilbert, March 6, 1858.

42. William W. Wolcott to S.W. Howard, March 1, 1882.

43. Toledo Commercial, January 6, 1873.

44. The Advance Era, May 6, 1905.

45. Smith, John, History of Maumee, p. 160.

*Excerpts from the correspondence between Wells family members can be found in the following:

    Rebecca Wells to Anne Wells Turner, December 6, 1812.
    Ann F. Wells to Rebecca Wells, December 25, 1816.
    Samuel Wells to Miss Rebecca Wells, February 26, 1817.
    Margaret Geiger to Rebecca Wells, March 27, 1817.
    Anne Turner to Rebecca Hackley, April 10, 1817.
    William Turner to Rebecca Hackley, May, 1817.
    Anne Turner to Rebecca Hackley, no date.
    Anne Turner to Rebecca Hackley, February 15, 1818.
    Ann Wells to Anne Turner, November 2, 1821.
    William Wayne Wells to Rebecca Hackley,
    February 27, 1828
    Jack Hackley to John and Jane Griggs, July 21, 1843.

For Further Reading

Published.

Alig, Joyce L. Ohio's Last Frontiersman, Mariner Captain, James Riley, Mercer County Historical Society, 1997.

Carter, Harvey Lewis, The Life and Times of Little Turtle, First Sagamore of the Wabash, University of Illinois, 1985.

Dawson, John W., "Charcoal Sketches of Old Times in Fort Wayne," Daily Sentinel, 1872.

Griffin, Robert C. and Alegre, Mitchell, Wolcott Family in America, 1986.

Griswold, B.J., The Pictorial History of Fort Wayne, Indiana, Chicago, 1917.

Hutton, Paul A., "William Wells: Frontier Scout and Indian Agent," Indiana Magazine of History, 74, (1978) pp 185-220.

Knopf, Richard C., Campaign Into The Wilderness: The Wayne-Knox-Pickering Correspondence, 1955.

Meuter, Hon. Maria Kitty, The Long Rifle, The Bow and The Calumet ,McClanahan Publishing House., 2000.

Parkins, James H., Annals of the West: Embracing a Concise Account of Principal Events Which Have Occurred in the Western States and Territories From the Discovery of the

Mississippi Valley to the Year, 1845. James Albach, 1847.

Smith, Dwight L., "William Wells and the Indian Council of 1793," Indiana Magazine of History, 56 (1954) 217-226.

Quaife, Milo M., ed., The Indian Captivity of O.M. Spencer, Citadel Press, 1968.

Volney, Constantin F., A View of the Soil and Climate of the United States of America, University of Illinois, 1968. (Original edition, 1840)

Walker, Joseph E., "Plowshares and Pruning Hooks for the Miami and Potawatomi: The Journal of Gerald T. Hopkins, 1804." Ohio History, 88 (1979) 361-407.

Wendler, Marilyn V., The Foot of the Rapids: Biography of a River Town, Maumee, Ohio, 1838-1988, Dariang Press, 1988.

Wendler, Marilyn V., Castles and Cottages, Historical Homes of Maumee, Ohio, Arcadia, 2002.

Wright, Richard J., ed., The John Hunt Memoirs: Early Years of the Maumee Basin, 1812-1835. Maumee Valley Historical Society

Unpublished
Journal of Nathan Rathbun, St. Paul's Episcopal Church

Wells File, Filson Club, Louisville, Kentucky.

Wells Family File, Fort Wayne Historical Society.

Wells Family Papers, Kentucky Historical Society

William Henry Harrison to William Wells, Ohio Historical Society

William Wells

Wolcott Family Papers and Letters, Lucas County/Maumee Valley Historical Society.

Wolcott Papers, Private Collection.

ABOUT THE AUTHOR

MARILYN VAN VOORHIS WENDLER served as the Director of the Lucas County/Maumee Valley Historical Society and Curator of the Wolcott House Museum Complex from 1990 through 1999. *The Kentucky Frontiersman, The Connecticut Yankee and Little Turtle's Granddaughter* received an Award of Achievement from the Ohio Association of Historical Societies and Museums in 1999. Additional publications include *Foot of the Rapids: The Biography of a River Town, Maumee, Ohio, 1838-1988* (Daring Press, 1988) which received an Outstanding Achievement Award from OAHSMA in 1988; *Images of Maumee* (Arcadia Press, 2000); *Cottages and Castles of Maumee*, an architectural history, (Arcadia, 2002) and numerous articles on state and local history. Ms. Wendler taught Ohio History at the University of Toledo from 1976 to 1990 and at Lourdes College, 1998 and 1999. She served as a member of the Board of Trustees of the Ohio Historical Society from 1980 to 1989 and 1993 to 2003. She is official historian for the City of Maumee.